Published in the USA in 2022 by Welbeck Children's Books Limited
An imprint of the Welbeck Publishing Group
Based in London and Sydney.
www.welbeckpublishing.com

Design and layout © Welbeck Children's Limited 2022
Text copyright © 2022 Larry Hayes & Rachel Provest
Illustration copyright © Chris Madden

Designer: Dani Lurie
Design Manager: Matt Drew
Executive Editor: Suhel Ahmed
Production: Melanie Robertson

Picture on page 111 © Flame of life/Shutterstock.com

ISBN: 978 1 78312 848 8

Printed in China
10 9 8 7 6 5 4 3 2 1

FSC
www.fsc.org
MIX
Paper from
responsible sources
FSC® C144853

Larry Hayes
Rachel Provest

Illustrated by
Chris Madden

MAX YOUR MONEY

EARN IT, GROW IT, USE IT!

WELBECK

Contents

Introduction

Do you ever wonder about money? What does it mean to have money? Why are some people rich and others poor? And how do you get your hands on money—lots and lots of it?

Some people seem to have the magic touch when it comes to money—they just seem to have loads of it. How do they have so much? Were they lucky? Or do they know something others don't?

Then there are people who just can't seem to keep hold of money. It runs through their fingers like water.

You've probably heard of people who have made a fortune buying and selling Bitcoins or making viral videos. And you also probably know people who spend their entire lives paying off credit card bills.

You might be wondering which one you are. Are you money smart? Or money clueless?

Money Clueless?

Which one are YOU?

The good news is that you can get money smart just by reading this book, gaining the kind of knowledge that will pay for this book a thousand times over. By developing that magic knack for money, you'll learn how to increase your wealth no matter what your current financial situation is. You'll learn smart ways to earn money, grow money, and use money. You'll get savvy about your personal finance and learn how to control money instead of be controlled by it. You'll discover what rich people know and everyone needs to learn.

Money **Smart?**

EASY LIVING

Once you learn to use money more effectively, you'll discover that money can be a real force for good, both for you and the world at large.

We can't promise money will make you happy, but not being able to use money wisely will almost always lead to misery. On the other hand, knowing the secrets of how to **Max Your Money** will make happiness a lot easier to come by.

What Is Money?

We know that money is what people use to buy things and pay for services. And it is also what we accept for selling our own things and services. But **what is money?**

Why are you happy to be paid in money when you sell that bike on eBay or work in a coffee shop? Why are you so pleased to accept rectangular pieces of paper and round pieces of metal, or see some numbers rise on a screen, in return for parting with real stuff or for expending all that time and effort serving customers?

WHY would you swap that bike for crumpled-up pieces of **paper??**

PROMISE TO PAY THE BEARER

The one thing that all money has in common is that it is backed up by A PROMISE.

It is a promise we make to each other to treat money as something that has value. So, anything holding that promise has monetary value. It could be a 10-dollar bill, coin, check, IOU, cryptocurrency, or a pile of gold. And because we know everyone else has made the same promise as us, we know that, in turn, we can swap that money—whatever its form—for something we want, which could be food, clothes, or a house.

TWO-WAY TRUST

A $50 bill probably costs about the same amount to make as a $5 bill, so why does it carry more value? The only reason it has the value of $50 is because of trust. We trust that paper money can be exchanged for things, and its value is whatever is written on it.

If Monopoly money held the same trust, it would become real money too—and a game of Monopoly would be a tenser affair!

A game of Monopoly about to turn into a real-life Clue scenario.

Why Use Money?

Historians reckon metal objects were first used as money from as early as 5,000 BCE. So why was money invented in the first place? There are two reasons: first, money is handy as a **means of exchange**.

In other words, people swap it for stuff, so they don't have to barter (swap) goods, which can be difficult if you don't have the right goods or if the value of your product isn't the same as what you want to swap it for.

THAT'LL BE HALF A COW PLEASE.

Paying for magic beans using a cow can be difficult.

Secondly, money is a **store of value**. This means it represents something valuable that is ready for when you need or want something in the future. Think about which is easier to keep and have ready to use as a means of exchange: some money or the cow?

JARGON BUSTER

Money is a store of value = you can save it to use later.

HOW TO GROW MONEY

Now that you know what money is, you're probably thinking: "Now take me to the good part. Show me how to make a lot of money quickly!"

How do I go from **this** to *this*?

There are two main ways to get money, you can either:

EARN IT by swapping your time, labor, and effort for money	**OR**	**GROW IT** by making the money you have do the work. This is through putting your savings into investments or using it to build a business.

If you are serious about becoming wealthy, you'll need to learn the secrets to both. Read on and we will reveal all!

Earn It

Work to Earn

Swapping our time, effort, sweat, and toil for money is how the majority of us make a living. Unless you are lucky enough to receive a large inheritance, the first way you will probably get your own money is through a paid job. While you're still at school, you might boost your wealth by doing chores around the house, helping your dad wash the car, or taking on a baby-sitting job.

Learning how to earn money as a kid is a great skill that will be good practice for the rest of your life. But, you can do better than that. Whatever your current financial standing, how about maximizing your wealth and happiness by earning the most money doing a job you enjoy? The other advantage about earning money as a kid is that everything you earn you get to keep. Think about it. You have your parents feeding you, housing you, providing your clothes, and paying for school trips. So, making money now is the chance of lifetime, because you have no bills to pay!

The question is how much can you earn? Some people earn more in an hour than others do in a month. Take a look at how much some of these professions pay:

WHAT DO PEOPLE EARN?*

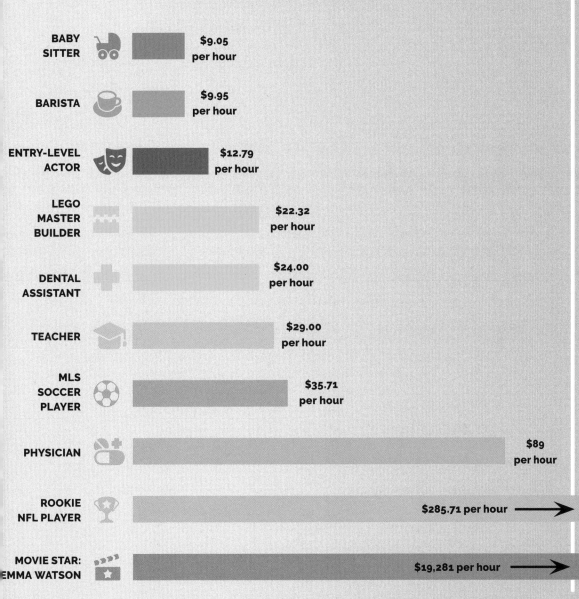

BABY SITTER	**$9.05** per hour
BARISTA	**$9.95** per hour
ENTRY-LEVEL ACTOR	**$12.79** per hour
LEGO MASTER BUILDER	**$22.32** per hour
DENTAL ASSISTANT	**$24.00** per hour
TEACHER	**$29.00** per hour
MLS SOCCER PLAYER	**$35.71** per hour
PHYSICIAN	**$89** per hour
ROOKIE NFL PLAYER	**$285.71 per hour** →
MOVIE STAR: EMMA WATSON	**$19,281 per hour** →

*Average pay depends on experience and vary by state; these are only for guidance.

Why Some People Earn More than Others

The price for people's time is mainly determined by one of the basic ideas of economics, known as **supply and demand**.

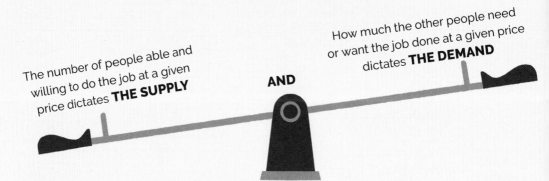

The number of people able and willing to do the job at a given price dictates **THE SUPPLY**

AND

How much the other people need or want the job done at a given price dictates **THE DEMAND**

For example, a football manager looking for a player with the ability to score big in the National Football League (NFL) will face a limited supply, because there aren't many superstar quarterbacks around. The demand for that player is high, because he will probably win games for the team, meaning huge financial rewards for the club.

Let's turn the tables. What if you need to employ someone to babysit? Well, there are a lot of kids trying to earn some extra cash. This makes the supply high, which lowers the hourly rate that any prospective babysitter can charge. Even the world's best babysitter would struggle to charge the average $285.71 hourly rate of a rookie NFL player!

So, what determines supply and demand?

SUPPLY LOW OR SUPPLY HIGH?

Supply can be LOW for many reasons. The job might be dangerous or unpleasant. It might require particular skills and qualifications that are hard to come by. Or it might just be that supply is low at certain times of the year or day (the cost of a taxi at 3 a.m. is usually more than double what you'd pay at 3 p.m.).

Some professions (such as lawyers, accountants, and physicians) keep supply artificially low by restricting the numbers of people who qualify each year. Alternatively, supply can be HIGH, because a job is somehow *desirable* (taxi driver due to flexible hours). Maybe it is low skilled (shelf stacker in a store) or fun (pet groomer). Maybe it provides a sense of well-being (yoga teacher) or status (politician) or job security (nurse) or maybe it's just cool (DJ).

DEMAND LOW OR DEMAND HIGH?

Demand can be low when there are easy alternatives to employing someone, such as using a robotic lawnmower instead of employing a gardener. There is also low demand for jobs that do not require much skill. Or maybe demand is low because the job is just not that important (such as a shoe-cleaning service).

Often, demand is high when it is important the job is performed to a high standard. No one, for example, ever types "cheap eye surgeon" into a search engine. But demand can also be high if there is a time pressure. Think about it—that locksmith is worth the $150 call-out fee when you're locked out on a rainy night and no plumber is too expensive when your toilet starts leaking uncontrollably!

Another big driver of high demand is where the employer happens to be a highly profitable company that can afford to pay top rates for good workers (the average salary at Google is about four times the U.S. national average).

Are the Huge Differences in Pay Fair?

Let's take another look at the chart on page 13 showing the average hourly rate of various professions. Let's try to understand why some jobs pay much more than others. After reading the arguments, which camp will you belong to–the one that believes the differences are fair or the one that thinks they are unfair?

Average teacher salary: **$63,645**

Professional soccer player yearly earnings (top 86 percent): **$384,204**

TEACHER VS. PROFESSIONAL SOCCER PLAYER

YES, IT'S FAIR!

1. Highly skilled soccer players are rare so deserve their high salary.
2. Soccer careers are short (average retirement age is 30) so they should earn a lot of money while they can.
3. Players face a high risk of injury so should be financially rewarded.
4. Top-level soccer brings a lot of happiness joy to society—that's why fans pay so much to see it.
5. The market sets the value—if the market doesn't decide who does?

NO, IT'S NOT FAIR!

1. Teaching is much more valuable to society than soccer.
2. A teacher gives a student the gift of knowledge, whereas a soccer player has little or no interaction with their fans.
3. Teaching is among the most economically important professions, because the future of any economy relies on the education of its youth, so teachers should be paid more.
4. It is crazy that a teacher earns more than six times less than a soccer player! We should tax a soccer player's income more than we do and put that money back into education.
5. A portion of the sponsorship income soccer clubs receive comes from gambling firms. Gambling is harmful to society— let's ban them and a soccer player's income will drop to a fairer level.

DO KIDS GET MINIMUM WAGE?

The minimum wage was invented so that adults can live on what they earn. The federal minimum wage for people under 20 is $4.25 for the first 90 consecutive calendar days. After that, it's the same as for adults: $7.50 per hour. However, state minimum wages may differ. Nevertheless, you can use the lessons in this book to blast right through the minimum wage! Turn over to the next page to learn how to maximize your earnings.

Max Your Earnings

If you want to maximize your earning potential, you will need to find work that has a low supply and is in high demand, plus it should be something that you enjoy doing. Which field of work appeals to you the most and what do you need to get started?

WHAT DO YOU LIKE?

MAKING THINGS

ETSY SHOP OWNER ($-$$$+)
Check out what's selling on Etsy and see if you can do better. Design a product that can be produced in bulk. Post a photo of it on Instagram to attract buyers.

VIDEO PRODUCER ($$$-$$$+)
Demand for videos is huge. Cheap or even free online video production courses can make you proficient in just a few months. Focus on your creative strengths when you're selling your services through a freelancer site.

RESEARCHING

GENEALOGIST ($$)
Freelance researchers can charge up to $2,700 for an ancestry report. Get a trial subscription to an ancestry website and use their free learning tools. Then, start selling your services on a freelancing site, such as Upwork or PeoplePerHour.

BUSINESS RESEARCHER ($$)
Businesses looking for a target list of customers go to freelancer sites for researchers. As a researcher, you must understand the client's needs, present the information clearly, and deliver on deadline.

$ = Minimum Wage | $$ = 2 x Min Wage | $$$ = 3 x Min Wage

ENTERTAINING

VOICEOVER ARTIST ($-$$$++)

Got a good talking voice? Then sign up with a freelancer site to get some gigs. And once you have some decent examples of your work, contact a voiceover agency. To get started, you'll need a condenser microphone, a pop shield, some headphones, and a quiet room.

VIDEO AD CREATOR ($$-$$$+)

Short video ads with viral potential are in huge demand. Working as a video ad creator can be lucrative. Ultimately, you can set up your own online ad agency or even start advertising your own business through viral videos. Sell your services on Fiverr and Upwork.

WHAT IS THE RIGHT JOB FOR YOU?

Start by asking yourself a few key questions. What do I like doing? What are my "sellable" skills? What type of work suits my personality?

And then look at it from the other end. Take a look at what jobs are out there. There are, literally, thousands of ways for you to earn money, so don't settle for something that undervalues your time and skills.

BEING ACTIVE

DOG WALKER ($-$$)

Dog ownership is at an all-time high. Volunteer with a local charity to get some initial experience. Advertise locally with hand-delivered flyers and build up a customer base. Research the local competition to set your rates.

LAWN TREATMENT PROVIDER ($$-$$$)

Get some training in lawn care (online courses are available) and rent the equipment initially. Check the local competition to set your pricing, advertise locally with leaflets, and you're ready to get started.

IMAGINING THINGS

LOGO DESIGN ($-$$$)

Taking a logo design course is a cheap way to acquire a new skill. Any design career will give you experience in managing and understanding a client's needs, wants, and expectations.

WEBSITE DESIGN ($$-$$$+)

Website design courses take some time, but they don't need to be expensive. This hard skill will be useful in any field of work. Get on a freelancer site and offer a freebie to get yourself known and have something to show potential clients.

Which Jobs Suit My Personality?

Sure, you can do a lot of things, but it's better to find a job that brings out the best in you. People who thrive in their profession are usually doing a job that suits them, so it does not feel like hard work. Think about what you are really like and try to find a job that suits both your character and personality.

 MAVERICK

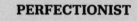 **PERFECTIONIST**

INFLUENCER ($-$$$++)

Many brands look for local personalities with a strong social media following. If this sounds like you, pick your social media platform, pick your area of interest—something you are passionate about—and get posting.

SOCIAL MEDIA MANAGER ($$-$$$+)

Many businesses hire freelance virtual assistants to manage their social media. Online courses are widely available to enhance your social media skills, helping you focus on creating content, driving sales, and finding the optimum route to fast growth.

PROOFREADER ($$)

A two-week, online proofreading course can give you a certified hard skill (see page 24) that will let you earn money regularly. You could sell your services through freelancer sites, such as textmaster.com.

VIDEO EDITOR ($$$-$$$+)

Software-specific video-editing courses are available onsite and online that run over from a few days to a few weeks. They oftern charge a fee, but a certificate will help to open of doors. Freelance opportunities are widely available on online jobs boards and freelancer sites.

$ = Minimum Wage | $$ = 2 x Min Wage | $$$ = 3 x Min Wage

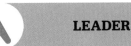

LEADER

CAMP ACTIVITY LEADER ($$)

Summer camps and kids activity programs need confident 16+ year olds to lead activity groups. If you've got what it takes to look after a group of younger children, this will be a fun way to earn money.

YOUTH SPORTS REFEREE ($$)

Most competitive youth sports, such as football, basketball, and baseball, need referees or umpires. If you're over 14, a natural leader, and enthusiastic about a specific sport, this can be the job for you. Each professional organization provides its own training courses.

HELPER

TUTOR ($$-$$$)

If you're 13 or above, you can take on tutoring jobs locally or online. Tutoring experience will help develop communication skills. Advertise locally, especially through parents or sign up with an online agency.

SWIMMING INSTRUCTOR AIDE ($$)

Even if you haven't received the appropriate swimming instructor certification, you can find work as a swimming instructor aide to help teach young children to swim. Work is flexible, well-paid, and can be rewarding.

COMPETITOR

GAMING COACH ($-$$)

You can literally earn money while playing your favorite game. Check the gaming section of freelancer sites, such as fiverr.com, and advertise your online coaching skills.

SEARCH ENGINE OPTIMIZER ($$$-$$$++)

Want to get a website on the front page of Google? A certified SEO course can give you a money-making skill. There is huge demand for SEO providers on freelancer sites and jobs boards, and, once you have a track record, earnings can really skyrocket.

ARTIST

ACTOR ($-$$$)

Enjoy performing? Join an acting class in the flesh or online. When you feel ready, start auditioning—and be prepared to audition a lot. Low-paid work as an extra is vital initial experience, so register with a reputable casting agency. Backstage.com is a good resource for performers.

ILLUSTRATOR ($$-$$$+)

Good at drawing? Then why not earn money from it? Earnings can be high if your style is sought after. Promote your portfolio on speciality creatives sites, such as Behance and Dribbble, and on social media, too.

Use Your Hard Skills

Let's look at your *Hard Skills*. These are qualifications and certified skills you can list on your résumé. Hard skills will take you into the big league when it comes to earning power. If you're eager to acquire a hard skill, you'll find most courses available online and often at a low cost.

WHAT ABILITY CAN YOU TURN INTO A HARD SKILL?

MUSICAL ABILITY

PROFESSIONAL MUSICIAN ($$$++)

If you're a talented musician and want to earn from music, enroll on an online music production course. E-learning sites, such as Coursera, Masterclass, and Udemy, offer high-quality courses. Once qualified, you can earn online by creating music and jingles for videos, podcasts, and audio books or by transcribing music, giving online music lessons, and mixing and mastering.

FOREIGN LANGUAGE FLUENCY

TRANSLATOR ($$-$$$)

Human translation services are still in demand and proofreading translation boosts your earning potential. Online assessments are readily available including from the globally recognized OECD (https://www.oecd.org/pisa/). A recognized qualification will bring you more work and allow you to charge higher rates.

TEACHING ENGLISH AS A FOREIGN LANGUAGE ($$$-$$$+)

The quality of TEFL courses varies, but even a short and inexpensive online course will get you started and let you see if teaching is for you. You can also sell your services through freelancer sites.

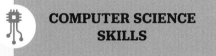 ## COMPUTER SCIENCE SKILLS

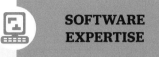 ## SOFTWARE EXPERTISE

CYBERSECURITY ($$$⁺⁺)

Defending computers and electronic systems from malicious attacks is big business. If you have enjoyed earning money with HackerOne.com, it could be time to take it to the next level. Earn much more than a minimum wage with a recognized Security Auditor certificate or a Cyber Security Incident Handler certificate. Even a Cyber Security Beginner Certificate can be valuable to customers of freelancer sites. There are several globally recognized institutes in this space with various price points for courses, including Microsoft, the ISACA, and the Global Information Assurance Certification.

CODER ($$$⁺⁺)

Whether you're skilled in Python, Java, or any other programming language, make sure you have an online course or certification behind you when you sign up to a freelancer site. A coding bootcamp site, such as Brainstorm or Treehouse, can give you credentials no matter what your skill level. Accredited coders typically earn 50 percent more than those without credentials or experience.

MS OFFICE SPECIALIST ($-$$)

Microsoft is still the world's most used software and freelancer sites are full of customers needing help with Office products (Word, Excel, Powerpoint, etc.). Holding a certified qualification will boost your earnings on freelancer sites. Microsoft provides its own Microsoft Office Specialist courses. But for a quicker and cheaper start, other websites, such as Udemy, offer specific software courses that will give your résumé credibility.

PHOTOSHOP EDITOR ($$-$$$)

Short, online courses are inexpensive and you'll recoup the cost as soon as you get your first job. Freelancer sites are the best place to advertise your services with a lot of work available.

MATLAB ($$$⁺⁺)

If you're a mathematics high flyer, MATLAB could turn you into a software programmer. Mathworks (the company behind MATLAB) runs its own proficiency certification program. Provable ability in MATLAB can be a shortcut to huge earning power.

$ = Minimum Wage | $$ = 2 x Min Wage | $$$ = 3 x Min Wage

Going on a Job Hunt

The final route to maximizing your earnings is to start looking at what jobs are available. Of course, it is a good idea to step out of the house and search locally, but in this digital age the big hourly rates are usually found online.

GO LOCAL

Check what jobs are available in your neighborhood. Ask around—start with your parents, grandparents, teachers, friends, and their parents. Let everyone know you're looking for work ideas and you will soon find that adults are full of them. There are plenty of jobs people will pay you to do, such as mowing lawns, painting and decorating, dog grooming, and car washing. People will even pay you to check on their house while they are away on vacation. You can also search for odd jobs in the local newspaper or advertised on flyers posted in the windows of local stores.

GO ONLINE

There are many online freelancer sites advertising jobs—these include fiverr.com, HackerOne.com, insolvo.com, and Upwork.com. Some require job hunters to be at least 13 years of age while others have a slightly higher minimum age requirement.

TOP TIPS FOR LANDING A JOB ONLINE

1. Browse the job categories and check the seller profiles. Also, see what services freelancers are selling in each category.
2. Make a list of every freelancer seller that catches your eye.
3. Next to each freelancer put down the hourly rate, total earnings, and any hard skills the job requires.
4. Just because you don't have the skills does not mean you can't acquire them. Free and inexpensive online courses are available in just about everything. Developing a hard skill is the single best thing you can do to maximize your earning potential.
5. If you are unsure where to start in a particular type of job category, contact a freelancer who is already working in that space. Ask them if they will be your mentor. Be ready with all your questions, and offer to help them on one of their jobs as an unpaid apprentice.
6. Getting the first job is always the hardest. Be prepared to offer a cheap introductory rate to get your first job.
7. Stay safe online—check the pointers on childnet.com. Ask a trusted adult if you're unsure about anything.

Boost Your Earnings

You can always boost your earning power, which not only means more money in your pocket but often less toil and more free time. The following tips will improve your chances of earning more.

1. **ENROLL ON COURSES** Even when you are qualified enough to do what you want to do, always aim to keep learning— whether formally through additional qualifications or self-study. Education is never wasted.

2. **LEARN A NEW LANGUAGE** On average, a second language equates to a 3 percent higher salary increase. That might not sound huge, but over the course of your working life it can mean a lot.

3. **FIND A MENTOR OR ADVISOR** As you grow in your work, you will meet similar people in the same field. You can fast track your success by learning from another person's experience. Asking someone to be your mentor can seem daunting; however, most people will be flattered, so don't be afraid to ask.

4. **TIME MANAGEMENT** If you are organized and efficient, it is easier to get a lot more done. Whether this is planning your day, prioritizing tasks, or finding better ways to do things, strong time management will give you an advantage over others.

5. **LEARN HOW TO SPEAK IN PUBLIC** Having the confidence to stand up and speak to people is a valuable skill. Strong communication skills will increase your chances of climbing up to a senior position. The fear of public speaking is believed to affect up to 75 percent of the population. Conquer this fear now and it will prove its worth over the years to come.

Want some inspiration on how to earn top dollar? Check these two money maxxers!

HOW I BECAME A TOP-PAID TUTOR

Tariq here! I'm 16 and I've been tutoring for two years. Being good with numbers, I now specialize in math tuition. Word has spread that I am a high-quality tutor, and so I have been able to increase my hourly rate considerably. In the future, I want to broaden my student base by going into online tutoring, and I will even consider setting up my own online tutoring agency. I am also planning on running coding courses for multiple children at once, using their coding projects as examples for promoting my courses.

MY RISE AS AN INFLUENCER

My name's Izzy and I am 15, I love reading and used #booktok to find recommendations on TikTok. I was surprised by the lack of decent YA book reviewers online. So I started posting my own book reviews and my following quickly grew. I am passionate about the books I review and make sure I engage with my audience and hashtag my videos. My video and editing skills have improved. The best thing I ever did was reach out to a similar reviewer and ask for their help and advice. I now have more than 50,000 followers. Initially, I was pleased to just receive free books, but now I've signed with an agency and earn substantially more from paid reviews and posts. I have now branched out onto Instagram to increase my earnings and review the occasional movie, app, and computer game.

Super Money Maxers:
Kids Who Nailed It!

Want some inspiration from kids who have made loads of money—and become celebrities in the process? These **Super Money Maxers** all made their fortunes in different ways, but they have a few things in common: they are hard workers who took a chance. But most of all, they are passionate about what they do.

MONEY MAX ENTREPRENEUR
Emil Motycka of Motycka Enterprises

Emil from Boulder, Colorado, started a lawn-mowing business at nine years old. At 13, he took out a $8,000 loan to buy a commercial lawn mower. By working hard and saving the money he made from mowing lawns, Emil was not only able to pay back the loan for the first lawn mower, but go on to buy a second. By hiring someone to run the second mower, his business continued to grow. Over time, Emil replicated this process until he had several mowers and employees, which allowed him to form Motycka Enterprises by the time he was 18. He went on to make well over $100,000 that summer. He is now making millions, with more than 60 employees.

MONEY MAX INFLUENCER
Evan of EvanTubeHD

Evan Moana from Pennsylvania started a YouTube channel called *EvanTube* when he was eight years old. He is now 15 and makes approximately $1.3 million a year from his channel, which has more than a million subscribers. His net worth (what he is worth in total) is estimated to be $12 million! What are his videos about? Things children his age are into: Minecraft, Angry Birds, and Lego! Sometimes being passionate about something is all you need to create something incredible.

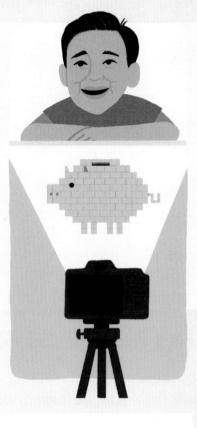

I'M THE TOP BUG BOUNTY HUNTER!

MONEY MAX HACKER
Santiago—the million dollar hacker

Santiago Lopez, from Buenos Aires, Argentina, is an "ethical hacker" who earned more than $1 million in rewards from HackerOne.com—a bug bounty platform that offers money for finding vulnerabilities in software systems—before his nineteenth birthday! Santiago taught himself all about hacking by watching YouTube videos and reading blogs. His strategy is quantity over quality, so he always looks for less severe bugs. His target is to find the highest value (in monetary terms) bugs in the least amount of time.

MONEY MAX VLOGGER
Ryan of Ryan's World on YouTube

At nine years old, vlogger Ryan Kaji from Houston, Texas, earned $29.5 million in 2020 from his "unboxing" YouTube channel, which has more than 22 million followers. He started after watching other toy review channels and asking his mom: "How come I'm not on YouTube when all the other kids are?"

His dad was already a YouTube vlogger, but when Ryan took things into his own hands, the big discovery was that videos with kids in them average three times as many viewers as those without. Just make sure your content appeals to adults, too, to avoid YouTube's "made for kids" policy, which restricts videos when under 13 year olds are the primary audience. To manage this, and help protect children from viewing unsuitable content, YouTube has developed a channel for children.

03:59 / 09:56

MONEY MAX ACTOR
Daniel Radcliffe of the Harry Potter movies

The hero of the Harry Potter movies earned $88 million before his twenty-first birthday! It's worth knowing that the demand for child actors is growing at 12 percent year on year. But before you start Googling "Acting Agencies for Children" you should also know that this is a tough industry to break into and the average unknown actor earns not much more than the minimum wage. Competition is strong and you need both extraordinary talent and luck to be noticed above the rest. Get into acting only if it is something you are truly passionate about.

MONEY MAXIMUS!

MONEY MAX WRITER
Christopher Paolini—child author extraordinaire

This precocious writer penned the first *Eragon* book at 15 years of age and initially self-published it. It was then picked up by Knopf Publishing, who turned it into a New York Times Bestseller, netting its author more than $1 million in the first six months. Paolini wrote another three books in the series. Interestingly, he was home-schooled and graduated at the age of 15, which perhaps gave him more time to write.

Got the Job, Now What?

Keep striving once you have landed the job. Think of it as the starting point to what you can earn. Now is the time to show your value to your customers or your employer.

Workers often assume that they are expected to be brilliant, which simply isn't true. In most cases, an employer wants to be able to trust you to get the job done. Below is a list of key areas in which you can demonstrate your professionalism and value as an employee.

FIVE KEY THINGS EMPLOYERS AND CUSTOMERS VALUE

1. **RELIABILITY** Just do the job. Forget the excuses; if you have no choice but to let someone down, let them know as soon as possible and say sorry.

2. **COMMUNICATION** Reply as soon as you can, let people know the best way to get in touch, and keep them updated on your progress.

3. **MANAGING EXPECTATIONS** The worst mistake you can make is to over promise and under deliver. Setting people's expectations too high usually ends with disappointment. When pitching, be realistic about what you can achieve.

4. **REALISTIC PRICING** While you might believe you are the best one for the job, there will always be others who can offer more or do the job for less. So, be competitive with your pricing; don't price yourself too high or too low. Too low a price might make a customer question the quality of your work/service.

5. **ABILITY TO LISTEN** Take time to understand your customers' needs. Customers sense immediately when somebody is just waiting for a break in the conversation so that they can launch into a sales pitch. Remember, it's about the customer, not about you.

HOW TO GET A PAY RAISE

Employers will rarely pay you more unless you are doing something better or offering more than what was agreed at the time of negotiation. Constantly reviewing the quality of your work will help you to make better decisions and ultimately earn more! Here are two top tips to keep you on track:

TOP TIP 1: SHOW YOUR PROGRESS

Make it easy for your employer (or even your teacher) to see the hard work you are putting in and your progress. Imagine how much effort an employer has to make when it comes to deciding who has done well out of many team members. So, help them by keeping a record of your efforts and achievements, plus the improvements you are making, By being able to share this with the decision maker, your chances for recognition and reward grow.

ERM, THERE
IS ONE OTHER
THING . . .

BOSS

2: KNOW YOUR WORTH

"If you don't ask, you don't get." When it comes to getting a raise, this is an important saying to remember. For every pay raise you don't ask for, or don't ask enough for, the gap between you and the person who is as good as you but *did* ask, grows. This is known as the compounding effect.

What About Your Career?

There are some things you can do *now* to pave the way for a high-paying career. A first step is understanding what career you will probably excel in. Remember your primary goal should always be to consider a career you will enjoy.

A career that will maximize your well-being will probably also make you realize your full earning potential. For example, if you are passionate about coding, you will probably earn more as a coder through career progression than if you become an actuary but hate the job—even though actuaries are highly paid. (In case you were wondering, actuaries are mathematical experts who use their skills to measure the probability of future events and predict the financial impacts these may have on businesses). Alternatively, if you love math and finance, a career as an actuary could be ideal for you.

But where do you even start? Let us help you. Find your perfect career with our Max Your Career action plan!

MAX YOUR CAREER

1. Take a personality test. Knowing yourself is the first step. But don't fall into the trap of thinking your personality is fixed. Personalities change over time, especially during our teenage years, and yours will also evolve through experience. See your personality test results as a starting point. Go to: https://www.ucas.com/careers/buzz-quiz

2. Take a careers aptitude test (and do it regularly as you continue to grow your skill set). These tests will give you ideas about possible career paths, which is half the battle. They will also help you focus on the school subjects that are important for the career paths that seem appealing to you.

3. Focus on your hard skills (see page 24). Whether you are in work or education there is always an opportunity to develop your skill set, especially with some extra online courses. Hard skills are like gold dust on a résumé. Develop skills you enjoy and they will pave the way to a great career. Remember, hard skills can be anything from a law degree or an online diploma in SEO marketing to learning how to mix music or even cocktails!

I KNOW THE PAY IS AMAZING, BUT I NEED A NEW JOB.

4. Get experience before your commit. Based on research interviews, this is the **Number 1 Tip** and failing to get experience is the **Number 1 Regret**! Use your family, friends, and even teachers (otherwise known as your network) to get some work experience. If you are 16 or over, look for local youth employment programs in your state that offer mentoring, opportunities for work experience, and even apprenticeships..

Earning Money in the Future

Technology has made thousands of jobs redundant over the course of history. And with advances in artificial intelligence (AI), while automation and robotics are getting ever faster, humans will need to adapt if they want to have successful, well-paid careers.

We have lived as . . .

WE ARE HERE

| Hunters | Farmers | Industrial Workers | Information Workers | What's Next? |

A NEW AGE DAWNS

Never have humans had so many possibilities to go anywhere, do anything, build anything, and become whatever they want to be. Your choices will make all the difference. Going to school, achieving good grades, obtaining a degree, and then landing a stable job at a company may have made sense 30 years ago, but this is a fast-changing world. The sun is setting on the information age as we enter the age of **Intelligent Technology**.

WHICH JOBS WILL PROBABLY DISAPPEAR?

The time when having a profession—and the speciality knowledge that went with it—was a safe route for earning a lot of money may soon be over. Before you get too excited about your future career, see whether the terminator is coming for your job before you are even old enough to apply for it.

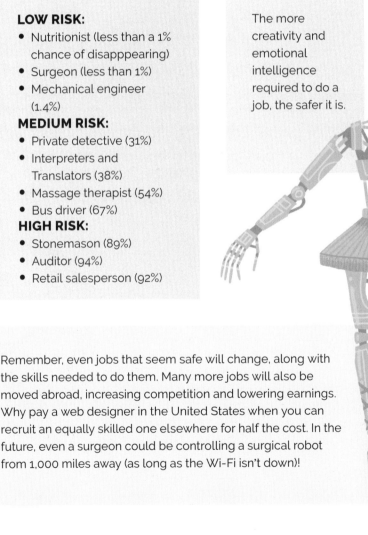

LOW RISK:
- Nutritionist (less than a 1% chance of disapppearing)
- Surgeon (less than 1%)
- Mechanical engineer (1.4%)

MEDIUM RISK:
- Private detective (31%)
- Interpreters and Translators (38%)
- Massage therapist (54%)
- Bus driver (67%)

HIGH RISK:
- Stonemason (89%)
- Auditor (94%)
- Retail salesperson (92%)

The more creativity and emotional intelligence required to do a job, the safer it is.

Remember, even jobs that seem safe will change, along with the skills needed to do them. Many more jobs will also be moved abroad, increasing competition and lowering earnings. Why pay a web designer in the United States when you can recruit an equally skilled one elsewhere for half the cost. In the future, even a surgeon could be controlling a surgical robot from 1,000 miles away (as long as the Wi-Fi isn't down!)

Some jobs are safe!

Jobs of the Future

History suggests that new jobs will emerge to replace the professions that are no longer needed or taken over by technology. Futurologists are already predicting new careers that will emerge over the next 10 to 15 years.

VERTICAL FARMER

Vertical farming is the practice of growing crops in vertically stacked layers, a little like building a tower in a game of *Jenga*. It uses special growing techniques that do not require soil. As land in urban areas becomes more precious due to rising populations—forcing people to build houses on land that were once used for farming—growing upward helps to ensure we don't run out of farmland. To become a vertical farmer, you will need expert knowledge of agriculture, as well as know what to grow, depending on who you are selling to and their food preferences. You cannot be scared of heights, either!

SPACE PILOT

Summer trips to space could soon become an option for the superrich, with companies such as Boeing, SpaceX, and Axiom Space planning to launch tourists to the International Space Station soon. So, the demand for spacecraft pilots could become among the highest-paid jobs on the planet. What does it take to become a space pilot? According to NASA, you will need:

- A Masters degree in a subject such as engineering, biological science, physical science, computer science, or mathematics.
- Two years of flying experience or at least have clocked up a 1,000-hour pilot-in-command time on a jet aircraft.
- The ability to pass the NASA long-duration flight astronaut physical.
- Skills in leadership, teamwork, and communication.

COMPANION FOR THE AGED

By 2050, the number of people 60 years old and over is expected to reach more than two billion globally. The number of years we live (also known as life expectancy) is steadily rising, thanks to technology, improved medicine, and better healthcare. However, with more old people in the world than young, who is going to look after them all? Becoming a companion for the elderly involves helping them with such tasks as cleaning and shopping or taking them for a walk. To do well in this career, you will need plenty of patience and need to be receptive to your clients' needs. Did you know that the Japanese have already developed a robot programmed to keep old people company? So, if this sounds like your dream job, you will need to make sure you offer better company than a robot.

EXTINCT SPECIES REVIVALIST

The estimate is that between 200 and 2,000 species die off each year, and this could increase as climate change worsens. While this is not good news for anyone, the technology exists to help bring extinct species back to life. From genome editing to extracting and synthesizing DNA strands, extinct species revivalists will soon be able to re-create lost animals and return them to their natural habitats. Think Jurassic Park!

To become an extinct species revivalist, you will need a strong understanding of biology, chemistry, and medicine. You will also need to think about the risks and rewards of bringing certain animals back to life. Perhaps some creatures are best left in the past?

"T-rex tamer"

Future-proof Yourself

How will you earn money when artificial intelligence (AI) can do everything from driving a truck to writing a legal contract? The answer lies in you—read on to find out.

With the world changing so fast, how do you prepare for the unknown? The good news is that the human species has what it takes not just to survive but to thrive in the future. The key to success is not to learn or work like a robot. The real robots will do all that. In the future, nothing will be more important than being human. You will still need those hard skills on your résumé, but the soft skills will make you stand out.

SECRET 1: BE PLAYFUL

To deal with the speed of change, we will have to constantly learn and adapt, known as "in-the-moment learning." This means you will need to be ready to explore and maintain a playful attitude, Don't become one of those old people who is scared of getting a new phone or a new app. Be more like the five year old who instead plays with it, exploring it with ease!

SECRET 2: BE CREATIVE

Hone your creativity. Give yourself a project and set about realizing it. It can be anything. A business? A Lego alarm clock that feeds you M&Ms for breakfast? A new type of cheese? Whatever you want to create, *go for it*. Turning an idea into reality is one of the great secrets to happiness, and the more you do it, the better you will become. Creative people often live the most fulfilled lives, and it is the creators who also tend to become the billionaires.

SECRET 3: BE RESILIENT

Can you cope when things go wrong? Or the rules change? What about when you just simply don't know what to do? Knowing yourself is half the battle. How do you bounce back? Do you go into problem-solving mode? Great if you do, but don't forget to reach out to friends and family for help, too. Or do you rely on support from others to bounce back? That is good, too, building and maintaining strong relationships is your special skill. Just remember to practice problem-solving by yourself when you can.

Don't worry if you feel you don't have much *bouncebackability*. Resilience is like a muscle— the more you test it, the stronger the trait will become. Start small: Next time you have a setback and just want to walk away, DON'T. Instead, reach out to friends or family and tell them how you feel and what you are afraid of. Ask them to help you solve the issue and see if you can do it together.

MAYBE I SHOULDN'T HAVE ASKED THE KING'S HORSES FOR HELP

WHAT'S NEXT?

So far, so good; no minimum wage for you. But just knowing how to earn a lot of money is only half the story. Did you know that most money is grown, not earned? Think about that. All those people going to jobs day after day, and yet more money is grown by people investing and building businesses than all those salaries put together.

If you want to increase your wealth, the real secrets are yet to come. Turn the pages to learn how to make your money do the work. How to **GROW IT**.

Grow It

Road to Wealth

No matter how much money you have now, learning the most effective ways to grow that sum will not only make you money smart but also give you a head start on preparing for the future.

> I HAVE ENOUGH FOR TODAY, BUT WHAT ABOUT TOMORROW?

Did you know that the sum of all the salaries in the world does not come anywhere near the amount of money people make by investing and building businesses? This is because of the massive potential there is to make money using the money you already have. So, if all you are doing is working for your bucks, no matter how well you are earning, you are missing out BIG time. People who have learned the art of *growing money* are the real money makers. Learn some key lessons in this section and you, too, will be way ahead of most people on the planet.

When you start looking at investment opportunities, you will see that there is perhaps a **magic money tree.** And it has many branches that allow for you to grow your money in all kinds of ways:

RENT

You loan out your assets for a limited period of time.

CAPITAL GAINS

You invest in assets that go up in value over time.

INTEREST

You lend your money, or deposit it in a bank, and get a guaranteed return.

DIVIDENDS

You invest in stocks and earn a share of the company's profits.

THE MAGIC MONEY TREE

BUSINESS VALUE

You create value in a business you can sell (see page 70).

JARGON BUSTER

Interest is the reward you earn at a particular percentage rate, when you let someone else have your money for a while. Most interest is earned from banks or other financial institutions when you deposit money with them. But in the past few years peer-to-peer lending sites (such as funding circle.com and zopa. com) have sprung up, letting you earn interest by lending your money to others.

This may all seem mysterious, but don't worry—we're about to learn how these things work.

Appreciate It

Over time *some* assets "APPRECIATE" (they go up in value) while *other* things "DEPRECIATE" (they go down in value). Knowing the difference between what goes up and what goes down will have a massive impact on your future wealth, because you can make informed decisions on what to invest in.

What do you currently spend your money on? Probably, it's items such as fashionable clothes, the latest piece of tech, or the coolest video game. This is probably because they make you feel good, and you can show them off to your friends. But, over time, the value of these things usually goes down. The superrich, on the other hand, spend a lot of their money on assets that increase in value over time. You, too, can increase your wealth by investing in things with the potential to grow in value.

SMARTEST BUYS OF 2010

Let's go back to the year 2010 and look at a few money-spinning assets we could have bought for about $750.

BRAND NEW IPHONE 4

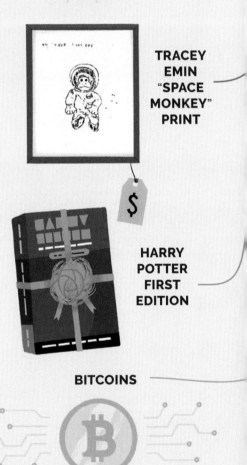

TRACEY EMIN "SPACE MONKEY" PRINT

HARRY POTTER FIRST EDITION

BITCOINS

TODAY'S VALUE: **$1,000**

The 16GB iPhone 4 cost $599 on release in 2010 and more than 200 million were sold globally over the next few years, and the tech is now well and truly obsolete. Unboxed, an immaculate iPhone 4 would now be worth about $1,000 as a collectors' item. But used? Not so much—they're available for about $30 on eBay.

TODAY'S VALUE: **$26,800**

Only 300 were ever made of these iconic Tracey Emin limited-edition prints. They first went on sale in 2009 at the Royal Academy in London and were still available to buy for as little as $650 in 2010. Tracey Emin has since secured her place in art history as a leading artist. Once an artist has created a legacy and secured a place in the canon of art history, their value rarely does anything but go up.

TODAY'S VALUE: **$1,350**

Harry Potter was already riding high in 2010 and the final movie was due out in 2011, when $650 would have bought you a first edition of the fourth book **Harry Potter and The Goblet of Fire**. Now that same book, *if you'd kept it in the same condition*, would be worth about double that. A copy signed by the author J.K. Rowling could bump the price up by about $13,500!

TODAY'S VALUE: **$50 BILLION**

Yes you hit the jackpot! Or maybe you forgot your passwords and lost the lot. If you'd invested $650 in Bitcoin in 2010 you could have bought as many as 886,000 Bitcoins. The value has been incredibly volatile over the past 10 years but, at the 2021 peak, they would have been worth $50 billion, making you the twentieth richest person in the world. (For more on cryptocurrencies see page 105.)

So, if you were to invest your money in an asset, how can you predict what will probably increase in value? There is no definitive answer, but a few principles will guide you. Go for anything that is in limited supply and you can keep in good condition. Avoid overspending on status tech and clothes.

But, remember, you don't have to just sit and wait for years. There are ways to make the value of your stuff go up *faster*. A lot faster.

Appreciate It *Faster*

So how do you boost the value of an asset? Let's take a look at some relatively simple things you can do to achieve this. Adding value to something can be surprisingly easy.

How to add value with a hammer

FIVE TOP TIPS!

1. GET A PHOTO

Buy an item of clothing that you have seen on a trending celeb. Then resell it, using a photo of that celeb wearing it, and with a 50 percent markup.

2. GET THE BOX

The value of a mint condition iPhone is double if it still has its box. If not, buy a replacement box online for about $10.

3. GET THE SET

A complete set of Harry Potter hardback books is currently worth about $200. Individually, you could pick them up for a third of that. So, a little effort to collect the set could result in you making a tidy profit.

4. GET THE AUTOGRAPH

A signed first edition of *Harry Potter and the Goblet of Fire* is worth $13,500—10 times that of an unsigned copy. So, to increase the value of your own favrite books, get them signed by the author.

5. GET IN FAST

Who doesn't want the latest pair of Nike Air Max sneakers? Preorder yours and ,as soon as they arrive, resell them for double the price on goat.com or stockx.com.

While these are some quick and easy ways to make money on assets you own, there is one key method used by money-savvy adults to boost their capital growth. It is known as "GEARING." Gaining a sound knowledge of gearing could help you to boost your wealth substantially when you are older. But gearing does come with risks, so you really need to understand how it works. Turn the page to find out.

It could be the most important lesson about money in this entire book!

Gear It Up

When you borrow money to boost an investment, it is called **Gearing**, because it's like putting your bike into a more powerful gear: you pedal less but harder and the bike goes faster. If you borrow to invest, your money does the same, it works harder. The results can be either spectacularly good or spectacularly bad. Let us start by looking at the perfect scenario.

Meet Jack, who in the year 2000 invested $10,000 in a house. He borrowed a loan of $190,000 (known as a mortgage) and bought a house for $200,000. Since then, he has only paid the interest on the loan, so he hasn't paid back any of the $190,000.

Value = $200k

I Owe the Bank = $190K

Although every year he pays interest on the mortgage, he no longer has to pay rent. And since interest rates have been low in recent years, it has been working out cheaper than paying rent, so Jack has more money to spend.

In fact, Jack has been using some of this extra cash to decorate and look after his property,

By 2021, this has happened:

The value of the house has grown by an average of 6 percent year on year. Over all those years that builds up to almost $700,000!

Value = $700k
I Owe the Bank
= $190K

JARGON BUSTER

A **mortgage** is simply the name of a loan you take out to buy a property. If you don't keep up your monthly repayments, however, the lender has the right to step in, take your property, and sell it to recover the money it is owed.

THE REWARDS OF GEARING

The $10,000 Jack started off with is now worth $510,000! In other words, his $10,000 has grown by more than 20 percent a year every year since 2000.

But there Is a second part to this, which is easy to forget so please pay attention. It is the dark side of gearing.

Gear It Up: The Dark Side

What if you gear up by borrowing too much? Well, if you buy a big house with a mortgage you can't afford to repay, the bank will soon repossess the house. There are other scenarios in which you might be tempted to borrow to invest, where the chances of crashing are far greater.

Gearing can cause a crash

Some investing and trading platforms let you gear up your money—they let you borrow to invest. Whether it's investing in companies or cryptocurrencies, the principle is the same. You borrow to boost your investment, but in these instances it is much harder to predict the outcome.

GEARING UP IN THE SHARE MARKET

You have $10,000 to invest. A trading platform lets you borrow $90,000 on top of this to invest a total $100,000 in the top 100 shares on the New York Stock Exchange (s NYSE).

If these NYSE shares, on average, have gone up 4 percent a year over the past 20 years—that means your $100,000 investment will go up by $4,000 in the first year alone. Even after you've paid interest on the borrowed money, you would still be in profit! So what could possibly go wrong?

A lot, if history is anything to go by. While some shares have risen in value, others have performed poorly. According to popular estimates, as much as 90 percent of people lose money in stock markets—this includes both new and seasoned investors. History also tells us that the market is often volatile, so it's difficult to avoid this roller-coaster ride even if you were to spread your investment across different shares. In fact, if you had geared up in the last 20 years, there are plenty of times when you'd almost certainly have gone bust.

THE COVID-19 CRASH

If you had invested the $100,000 at the start of 2020, on March 16 you would have witnessed the Dow Jones losing 12.9 percent and the NYSE suspending trading as a result of the COVID-19 pandemic. In order to keep paying interest on the borrowed sum, the investing platform would have forced you to sell everything at a massive $30,000 loss. You would have lost your original $10,000 and been left owing them another $20,000 on top!

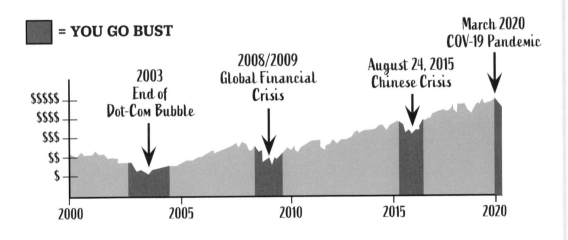

■ = **YOU GO BUST**

March 2020
COV-19 Pandemic

2003
End of
Dot-Com Bubble

2008/2009
Global Financial
Crisis

August 24, 2015
Chinese Crisis

$$$$$
$$$$
$$$
$$
$

2000   2005   2010   2015   2020

GEAR UP OR NOT?

Gearing up some investments, in moderation, can be great. For example, getting on the housing ladder early in life is almost always a good idea, because increasing demand in housing will probably drive up house prices in the long run. But beware of gearing up on other less predictable investments.

Rent It Out

Earn an income from your assets by renting them out. By doing so, you are effectively "boomerang selling," because your asset comes flying back, ready for you to rent it out again and again.

You can earn money on a regular basis in the form of rent on anything, from houses, vehicles, drones, camera lenses, and musical instruments to ice cream vans and storage space. Rental sites, such as FatLlama, help you to rent out almost anything. You, too, can earn your share of that rental income.

BUILD UP YOUR RENTAL CATALOG

Check FatLlama.com and see if you own anything that could be rented out. Once you start you may want to build up more assets. See what is renting locally and the rental prices. Can you buy that item cheaply, second hand on an online marketplace, such as eBay or Etsy? For example, a used drone that sells online for $300 but rents out on FatLlama for $30 a day.

RENT IT OUT FOR $30 A DAY!

Wear and tear is inevitable when you start renting out stuff, so make sure you save up a portion of the rental income until you've covered your cost price. Afterward, the rest is profit. Another tip is to take photos of your items each time you send them out. You can then claim on the site's insurance if your item comes back damaged or broken.

PREPARE FOR THE BIGGEST

Housing rent can be a huge source of rental income. When it comes to superboosting your earnings, renting out a property could be among the best financial decisions you ever make. Usually, the earlier you get on the housing ladder, the better. So in the future, as soon as you have a regular job, even if you're happy living with your parents or renting somewhere with friends, email a mortgage broker and talk to him or her about a mortgage. This is a loan for buying a property— make sure any repayments are more than covered by the potential rent. You'll need good advice about what to buy, where to buy, and how to look after your property, because there are risks with buying a property; the value of houses can go down, tenants may stop paying the rent, and, of course, there may be problems with furnaces, plumbing, and electrics that are costly!

Save It

The securest way to grow your money is to deposit it in a bank. Leave the money for a long time in an account that pays a decent interest rate and your savings will grow exponentially, thanks to the magic of **compound interest**. Take a look at this lucky baby girl, who has received a birthday gift of $1,000. The money is put into a savings account where it earns 5 percent interest a year:

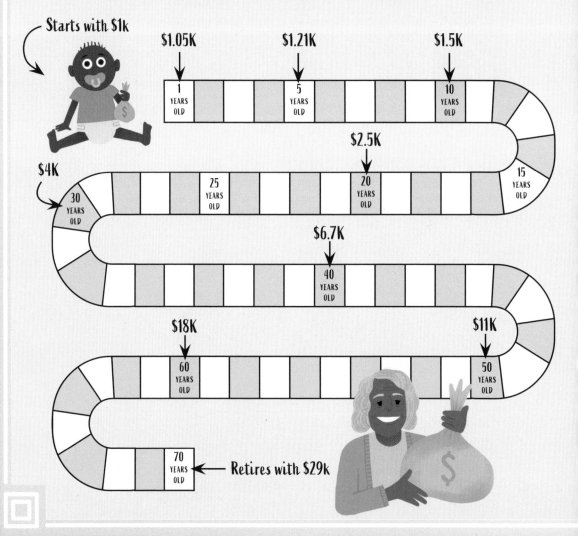

Starts with $1k

$1.05K — 1 YEARS OLD

$1.21K — 5 YEARS OLD

$1.5K — 10 YEARS OLD

15 YEARS OLD

$2.5K — 20 YEARS OLD

25 YEARS OLD

$4K — 30 YEARS OLD

$6.7K — 40 YEARS OLD

$11K — 50 YEARS OLD

$18K — 60 YEARS OLD

70 YEARS OLD ← Retires with $29k

By leaving the $1,000 in a savings account, the person is sitting on almost $29,000 by the time she retires. But for compound interest to work its magic, it needs both **time** and a **decent interest rate**. And at the current time, interest rates around the world are incredibly low.

So low, in fact, that if the baby saved their $1,000 at the current best available savings rate of 2.5 percent per year, their retirement fund would be worth only $5,500! Nowhere near the $29,000 that a 5 percent rate yielded.

$29K

$5.5K

Actually, it is even worse than you think. Because in 70 years time, that $5,500 won't be worth as much as it is now. Every year, money is worth less and less, because prices keep going up due to inflation. Understanding the impact of inflation on your money is important. And it's easy to misjudge it.

If you want your money to work harder to earn you more money, you can't just save—you need to start *investing* it.

JARGON BUSTER

Inflation is the rise in the prices of stuff over time. Every year any amount of money is worth a little less in terms of what it can buy.

Invest It

If you choose to *invest* your money instead of depositng it in a bank, you increase your chances of earning more—although things do get riskier. Make a bad investment and you can lose some or even all of your money. But more risk also means bigger returns (if things go well). And with better returns, compounding can really work its magic.

Although you need to be 18 or above to start investing, there are plenty of accounts your parents can open on your behalf and make trades for you. So, let's start with the biggest investment opportunity of all—**the stock market**.

JARGON BUSTER

An **investment** is an asset (such as a house or company shares or even a painting) that you put money into in the hope that it will grow in value, so that you can sell it for a larger sum of money.

THE STOCK MARKET

This is a place where people buy and sell shares, or little parts of companies. Companies offer these shares for sale so that they can get money to improve their businesses.

If you buy shares in a company, you can earn money in two ways. First, companies pay out a "dividend" to shareholders based on the profits they make. They sometimes pay out once a year, sometimes more often.

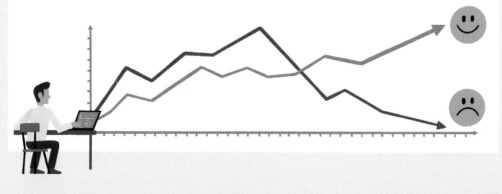

Secondly, the value of your shares can go up. In the future, if the company is doing well, or there's some good news about its future prospects, investors might be happy to pay more for the shares you own. The combined sum of dividends and share price gains equals your "total return" from owning a share.

But with investing there's a catch—investments can do down as well as up. Let's see how you would have fared in 2021 if you had bought shares in any of the four companies below in 2010.

WHICH COMPANY WOULD YOU INVEST $1,000 IN?

BP	**NOKIA**	**ROLLS ROYCE**	**AMAZON**

BP	NOKIA	ROLLS ROYCE	AMAZON
British Petroleum (BP) was pumping four million barrels of crude oil a day in 2010. But a disaster in April resulted in five million barrels ending up in the Gulf of Mexico. The business did recover, but never back to predisaster levels. In 2021, you're left with **$742**.	By 2010, low prospects for the cell phone company had sent its share price tumbling. Maybe you invested thinking the company would bounce back? Wrong. It fell further. In 2021, your $1,000 is worth only **$408**.	In 2010, Rolls Royce was making some of the world's most advanced jet engines. But in 2020 the COVID-19 pandemic destroyed its airplane engine earnings. With air travel still struggling in 2021, your $1,000 is down to **$449**.	In 2010, Amazon was making a loss! Money was being sucked in to build more warehouses and data centers. Amazon is now the world's *most valuable company*. In 2021, that $1,000 you invested is worth a whopping **$26,513**.

Of course, hindsight wonderfully reveals what choices should have been made in 2010. But let's look at the future. Will Rolls Royce shares bounce back up as soon as air travel returns to normal? Will Amazon struggle to grow anymore now everyone is already using it? No one can predict the future, but you can improve your chances of profiting from dealing in shares by learning a few golden rules. Turn the page to find out what these are.

The Golden Rules of Investing in Shares

Buying and selling shares isn't for the faint-hearted. People who work in the finance industry use their honed analytical and research skills to make sound investment decisions. What's more, there are a lot of books written about how to succeed in the share market. Once you are old enough to trade in shares, sticking to these five golden rules will help you in an unpredictable marketplace.

GOLDEN RULES

5 GOLDEN RULES OF INVESTING IN SHARES

1

DON'T PUT ALL YOUR EGGS INTO ONE BASKET

Spread your money across a variety of shares to ensure you don't experience too great a loss if one or two of your investments perform poorly. The more you diversify, the lower your overall risk. Even the biggest companies can crash unexpectedly.

2

REMEMBER THAT MARKETS ARE SMART

Assume the market is getting the value of a company about right. If a company looks really cheap, there's usually a good reason. So don't try to second guess a bargain. It's better to do your research and pick a promising company at a fair price than chase after every hot tip.

3

BUY TO THE SOUND OF CANONS

You might think the start of say, a war, or pandemic would be a terrible time to buy shares. But it's not. Buying shares after the COVID-19 pandemic struck would have made you a profit. The stock market rose just two days into the COVID-19 lockdown crash because the future impact of the pandemic started to become clearer from that point in time. So remember, the market is always looking ahead, and so should you.

4

BE A DRIP FEEDER

Drip feeding your money into shares over months and years is a great way to manage risk. The stock market is volatile, and, if you put all your money into it just before a crash, it could take years to recoup your cash. But if you invest month by month, year on year, you'll be in a better position to leave the money in for a longer period and can worry less about booms and busts.

5

DON'T BE A SHEEP

Don't just follow the flock. Know what you're investing in. You would be amazed how many people don't do any research. They hear a positive rumor about a company and decide to jump straight in. If you're serious about profiting from shares, first do some research on the company. Remember, the more you know about a company, the better your decision to invest will be.

DO A TEST RUN

Try fantasy investing and earn real cash prizes on apps such as invstr.com and fantasystockexchange.biz. For investing ideas and research, try reading moneyweek.com, wsj.com, or economist.com.

The Ways of an Investing Guru

THE SAGE OF OMAHA: WARREN BUFFET

Warren Buffet is possibly the greatest investor of all time. At the age of 10, after reading a book called *One Thousand Ways to Make $1,000* (it was the *Max Your Money* of its day), he started earning money selling chewing gum and magazines door to door. His first investment wasn't in shares. Instead, he bought a pinball machine and charged people for playing on it. That's when the money started rolling in.

He bought his first shares in 1942, at the age of 11, and became the world's richest person in 2008 with a fortune worth $62 billion. In 2021, Forbes listed him as the world's sixth richest person with a net worth of $96 billion.

So what are the secrets to his success?

TRY TO BE FEARFUL WHEN OTHERS ARE GREEDY AND GREEDY ONLY WHEN OTHERS ARE FEARFUL.

IF YOU AREN'T THINKING ABOUT OWNING A STOCK FOR 10 YEARS, DON'T EVEN THINK ABOUT OWNING IT FOR 10 MINUTES.

THE INVESTOR OF TODAY DOES NOT PROFIT FROM YESTERDAY'S GROWTH

INVESTING VERSUS GAMBLING

You have probably heard people say that trading on the stock market is just like gambling. In fairness, the two have some things in common. Luck does play a part in investing. There's risk and reward for sure, and fortunes can be won or lost. The major difference is that if you invest responsibly and steadily, then most of the risk can be managed.

The lesson you really need to learn, as early as possible, is that you don't need to take big investment risks to build your fortune.

Aside from investing, there are other, even faster ways to grow money. Remember the pinball machine that got Warren Buffet started? Well, you can do something similar. You just need to work with your assets to see some supergrowth.

Work Your Assets

Have you considered the earning potential of your assets? Spend a little time thinking about how you might use the things you already own to make money, and plenty of it!

ASSETS + WORK = SUPEREARNINGS!

Remember **Emil Motycka** (see page 30) who made more than $100,000 in one summer from mowing lawns? He started out simply mowing lawns for $7.50 an hour. It was only when he took out a $8,000 loan and bought his first commercial mower that he supercharged his earning power.

He could have simply rented it out and earned a little cash that way, but instead he used it. He used it to increase the amount he could earn.

Emil earned the minimum wage mowing lawns.

EMIL = $7.50 PER HOUR

But after he bought a commercial mower, he could earn four times as much.

EMIL + COMMERCIAL MOWER = $28 PER HOUR!

He could provide a service only adults were offering but at a cheaper rate. He was selling not just his time and effort, but a service that was in demand. And then came the really big step. He bought a second mower. Suddenly every friend at school was a potential employee and source of extra income to Emil. He could pay friends $14 per hour, leaving him an extra income of $14 on top of the income he was already making from operating his first mower. Suddenly the earnings went through the roof.

So, if you don't want to settle for miminum wage either, try some of these ideas.

WINNING COMBINATIONS

SELLING ICE CREAM $
+ ICE CREAM BIKE = $$$+

Work in an ice cream stand and you'll earn minimum wage. But buy (or rent) an ice cream bike and you can earn four times as much.

GARDENING $
+ STRIMMER = $$$

Offer to do some gardening and you'll earn minimum wage. But invest in a strimmer and you can earn three times as much.

CLEANING $
+ PRESSURE WASHER
+ TELESCOPIC GUTTER
LANCE = $$$+

Cleaning windows won't make you a fortune. But invest in some equipment and you can earn four times as much cleaning people's gutters, too.

$ = Minimum Wage | $$ = 2 x Min Wage | $$$ = 3 x Min Wage

In all the above examples, the addition of some useful equipment, or asset, effectively turns a service into a money-spinning business. Through the ages, it has been the successful entrepreneurs, or businesspeople, who have gone on to become some of the richest people in the world. Turn the page to find out how they got there.

The Ways of the Richest Person in the World

Whether it is Elon Musk, Jeff Bezos, or Bill Gates, there is a single reason why they are on the world's richest people list. Sure, they all set up successful businesses, but that's not the secret. The secret is that those businesses are worth much more than all the money they have ever earned. Sounds crazy, right?

Let's take a look at the world's current richest person: Jeff Bezos. He has a net worth of $201.7 billion, thanks to his 10 percent stake in Amazon Inc.—the company he founded, The whole company is estimated to be worth $1,7 trillion. But over the years, the company has not made anywhere near that much money. To date, Amazon's profits add up to about $47 billion, which is a tiny fraction of what it's worth. So, why is the company worth so much more than the money it has generated?

The secret is simple: When you build a business, you're building a money-making machine. And with any money-making machine, people are interested in how much money it is predicted to make in the future.

How much is a money-making machine worth? If people think that a business can make a lot of money in the future, they see it as a great investment and are prepared to pay a lot for it.

After spending years building up its warehouses and databases, Amazon is forecast to earn a lot of money next year, and even more the year after. In fact, some estimates suggest that the company could be worth more than $12.7 trillion by 2030!

WHO ARE THE RICHEST PEOPLE IN THE WORLD IN 2021?*

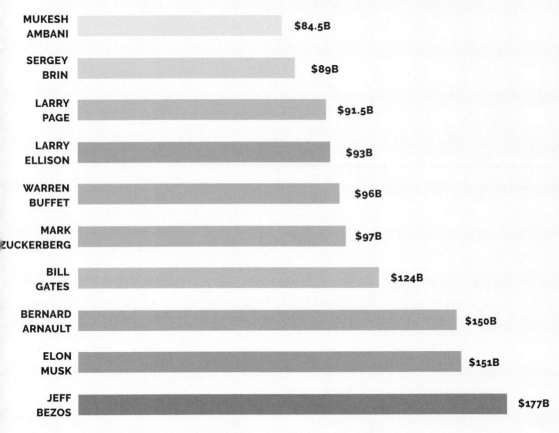

Name	Net Worth
MUKESH AMBANI	$84.5B
SERGEY BRIN	$89B
LARRY PAGE	$91.5B
LARRY ELLISON	$93B
WARREN BUFFET	$96B
MARK ZUCKERBERG	$97B
BILL GATES	$124B
BERNARD ARNAULT	$150B
ELON MUSK	$151B
JEFF BEZOS	$177B

* Taken from the 35th annual Forbes list of the world's billionaires. Figures denote net worth.

BECOME THE NEXT BEZOS

So, what has Amazon's fortune got to do with you? Well, in the past, selling your business was difficult. You had to hire a costly investment banker, who would help you to sell your company on a stock market. But now, thanks to the Internet, anyone can build and sell their own money-making machine. Let's take a look at how this is possible.

Build Your Own Money-making Machine

Anyone can sell a portion of their business these days, thanks to the wonders of Crowdfunding. Crowdfunding is when a person attracts a lot of small investors to buy into their entrepreneurial vision, typically by using a crowdfunding website.

There are many well-known crowdfunding sites, such as kickstarter.com, indiegogo.com, crowdcube.com, and crowdfunder.co.uk. The only snag is that you need to be 18 or above to use these sites, although you could always team up with an adult. Fortunately, the last few years have also witnessed the emergence of crowdfunding platforms, such as kideverest.com and gofundme.com, that cater for young entrepreneurs.

Want some inspiration? Let's take a look at one entrepreneur, 28-year-old Californian Palmer Luckey, who took the crowdfunding route to turn his vision into reality.

PALMER LUCKEY

Luckey started a project making a virtual-reality headset in his parents' garage when he was 15 years old. A few years late, he was ready with a prototype product—the first Oculus Rift Headset.

But Luckey was still at school and didn't have any money to manufacture a sellable product. So, he sought investment on the crowdfunding website Kickstarter.

For $300 he offered investors a build-your-own virtual-reality headset kit.

He was aiming to raise $250,000 but ended up with $2.4 million. It was among the most successful campaigns in the history of crowdfunding.

The money was used to fund the kits and develop a better product. Within two years, he had a cutting-edge, virtual-reality headset. By then, he had spent just about all of the $2.4 million, but what he had created was much more valuable.

He had created a top-quality product, a brand name everyone knew about, and the promise of huge future earnings.

Facebook decided all that was worth $2 billion so bought the patent and Palmer Luckey became a billionaire.

So what do you need to launch a business on a crowdfunding site? How do you even start building a business? Like everything else, it starts with an idea.

Brilliant Business Ideas

The best ideas start by identifying a problem and seeing it as an opportunity to find a solution. Or thinking of something that could be done better, quicker, or cheaper. Here are a couple of our favurites:

KINDLING CRACKER

After New Zealand teenager Ayla Hutchinson saw her mother almost lose a finger while splitting kindling with a hatchet, she set about trying to develop a safer solution. She came up with the Kindling Cracker— a cast-iron cage that holds the wood in place while you split it into pieces. There are now tens of thousands of Kindling Crackers being used in New Zealand and North America. Hutchinson said of her invention: "It gives people with disabilities or physical impairments the freedom to cut their own kindling again . . . It makes it easier and safer for everyone to cut kindling."

FLOW HIVE

Have you ever tried to get honey out of a beehive? Well Cedar Anderson, from Australia, heard his dad complaining about being stung all the time. With his father's help, Anderson spent years in a garden shed developing the Flow Hive—a beehive that delivers honey with the turn of a tap. He then went on the crowdfunding site Indiegogo.com, aiming to raise $70,000 for tools to help production. He ended up receiving nearly 38,500 orders from more than 130 countries and raising more than $12 million.

SPOT THE PROBLEM, FIND THE ANSWER

If you look around your house or workplace, you will probably see a huge number of problems or dull jobs that could be made easier by a new product or service. If you find a common problem that someone else hasn't already solved, chances are there will be a market for it.

Need help coming up with an idea? Try these two top tips:

TOP TIP 1

ASK PEOPLE

Ask your grandparents what they find difficult now that they are getting older. You could even ask your parents what makes their lives hard and think of how you could make it easier. Better still, ask people if they have any great product ideas that they have been too lazy to try out. You'll be amazed how many people have an idea they have done nothing with.

TOP TIP 2

BUILD SOMETHING BETTER

The solution doesn't need to be original. In any market, there's room for more than one product or service, and in most there's room for loads. Remember, Facebook wasn't the first social network, and Google wasn't the first search engine. Amazon wasn't even the first website to sell books. So if you see something working in a different country or a different town, think about how you might make it better. And then try it in your country or home town.

But what do you with your idea? How do you even know if it's a good one? Turn the page to find out.

Is It a Good Idea?

Some people have business ideas all the time. The difficult part is knowing which ideas to drop and which ones to go with. With any business idea, it's important to assess whether it is any good before you put in all that effort to get it off the ground.

The easiest way to test the strength of an idea is to ask yourself a few key questions. The answers will tell you all you need to know.

IS IT A GOOD BUSINESS IDEA?

WHY?

WHY ARE YOU DOING THIS?
You have a better chance of succeeding if it is something you feel passionate about. It shouldn't just be about making money.

Flow Hive founder Cedar Anderson is passionate about bees. Bees around the world are disappearing, and he wants to reverse that.

WHAT PROBLEM ARE YOU SOLVING?
Write down the problem in one sentence. If you can't do that, maybe the problem won't be clear enough in your customers' minds either.

Cedar Anderson grew up on a bee farm, where his dad was often stung by stressed bees when he opened up the hives to collect honey. The stress also caused whole hives to fall prey to disease. With the invention of Flow Hive came the promise of "tapping honey straight from the hive without opening it."

WHAT?

WHO ARE YOU SOLVING THIS PROBLEM FOR?
Track down some potential customers and ask them if they recognize the problem you've found, and ask them what they think of your solution.

WHO?

The Flow Hive sounded like a terrible idea to professional beekeepers. They weren't impressed and worried they would get less honey per hive. But, when Anderson talked to amateur beekeepers, they loved the idea. Honey on tap and with none of the complications. Who cares if there's a little less honey? Cedar had found his target market: **amateur beekeepers**.

HOW ARE YOUR COMPETITORS SOLVING THE PROBLEM TODAY?
This can be the hardest aspect to research, but you need to research your competition. Sure, you can ask people, but often they won't know that there's already a solution out there. So get on the Internet and start looking for solutions and competitors that already exist.

HOW?

Flow Hive was original. Before it came along, beekeepers were using the techniques they'd used for centuries.

HOW MUCH _PROFIT_ CAN YOU MAKE?
As part of planning your business, it's worth looking at the numbers right at the outset. Calculate both the cost of making your product and the price you think people will be willing to pay for it. That way, you can figure out the profit on every sale.

Remember that costs vary, depending on the number of sales you make. Some costs are "fixed" (they stay the same irrespective of the number of sales) and some are "variable" (the costs vary, depending on the number of sales you make).

PROFIT?

**WILL THIS BUSINESS
HAVE *VALUE*?**

Once you've established your business, will you need to keep it running in order to continue making money? Or could you, some day, sell the business? It makes sense to build value into a business so that in the future you have the option of selling it to prospective buyers and increase your wealth.

Flow Hive is Anderson's life passion. The idea of selling up isn't part of his thinking. But the option is there if he ever changes his mind. This is because he has established a profitable business, with patents to protect his ideas, and a brand name that is recognized globally.

Flow Hive's variable costs—such as the materials required to build the units—were fairly low. But the business also had some high fixed costs; for example, Anderson had to buy an injection mold for making the plastic honeycomb that cost about $50,000. The only way the Flow Hive made business sense was if he could sell a lot of them. That's why he went to Indiegogo. Now that more than 40,000 units have sold worldwide, the cost of the mold works out at around $1 per hive!

VALUE?

So, you have checked your business idea thoroughly and think it's a winner. Now what? How do you get your business idea up and running?

Test Your Business Idea

The best way of starting a business is to think of it as one big experiment. This means testing your idea every step of the way and only moving forward with the product/service if the results are positve. So, what's the first step in testing your business idea?

No matter whether your business idea is product- or service-based, you need to reach the point where you can test it on your target customers. For that, you need something often called a **minimum viable product**. This is the most basic form of your product that captures the essence of your idea.

LESS EQUALS MORE

Remember the story of the teenage entrepreneur Palmer Luckey (see page 70). He was working in his parents' garage to build a virtual-reality headset. He was confident people would love his headset.

But there was a problem.

He didn't have enough money to make his product. So he had to run an experiment to find out whether people would love his VR headset. For this he needed a minimum viable product.

He realized he could sell a lesser form of his device—a kit for making your own headset—that would be cheaper to manufacture but still get the idea across.

But it still wasn't cheap enough.

And then he figured he didn't even need a kit! His minimum viable product could just be a video showing what his invention could do.

"Pay me $300 now," said Palmer, "and I'll use it to develop the kit." And guess what? About 10,000 people did that.

HOW GIANTS ARE BRED

The world's largest companies started out this way, too. For example, the file-sharing service, Dropbox, started off as just a video demonstrating its capabilities. The creators asked people to sign up before there was even a company website.

Amazon.com was initially set up to sell books. It was four years later that Bezos started selling other items, once he had learned that customers really valued the convenience and reliability his site offered them.

Currently, Bezos is building his Blue Origin space company. In 2021, he tested his minimum viable product—a 10-minute excursion to the edge of space. How the venture will grow remains to be seen.

Developing the minimum viable product is just the start of the experiment. There's a way to go before you're ready to launch your business.

Lean Up Your Business Idea

Let's take the Flow Hive business idea and put it in the Lean Start-Up Machine. It's an experiment where we **BUILD** a minimum viable product, **MEASURE** how well it does, and then **LEARN** what to do next. And then we do it all again, making improvements all the time.

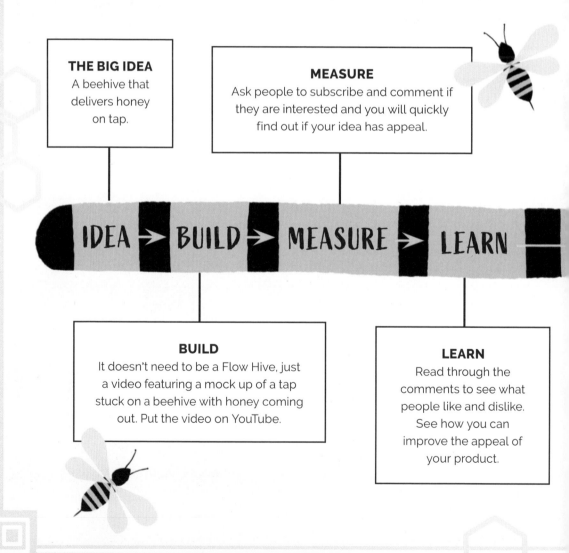

THE BIG IDEA
A beehive that delivers honey on tap.

MEASURE
Ask people to subscribe and comment if they are interested and you will quickly find out if your idea has appeal.

IDEA → BUILD → MEASURE → LEARN

BUILD
It doesn't need to be a Flow Hive, just a video featuring a mock up of a tap stuck on a beehive with honey coming out. Put the video on YouTube.

LEARN
Read through the comments to see what people like and dislike. See how you can improve the appeal of your product.

BUILD

Make a kit. Something that can be used to put a plastic honeycomb and a tap in an existing beehive. Sell it for a fair price, using the YouTube Channel, and ask for feedback.

LEARN

Cost can be cut by manufacturing in bulk. To achieve this, Anderson needs the help of a crowdfunding platform, such as Indiegogo, where he can access both money to invest in cheaper manufacturing *and* customers to buy his product.

BUILD ➤ **MEASURE** ➤ **LEARN**

MEASURE

The inventor of the Flow Hive, Cedar Anderson, receives the feedback. The market loves the idea but thinks the kit is too expensive.

THE 3 KEYS TO THE LEAN START-UP METHOD ARE SIMPLE:

1. Treat it as an experiment: You're in a constant loop of Building–Measuring-Learning.

2. Forget perfection and just do it: If in doubt, get out there and try to sell it.

3. Learn what customers value: Use feedback to develop your product.

If you have an idea, get out there and experiment. There's just one last thing you need to know before you start. If you have a really good idea, it might need protecting so that others can't copy it.

Protect Your Idea

Every now and then it's worthwile to first legally protecting your idea. You have probably heard of patents and copyright, trademarks, and design rights. If not, here is a quick jargon buster to get you started.

WHAT IS IT AND HOW DO YOU PROTECT IT?

WORK OF ART ➔ COPYRIGHT

You've written a book or an amazing piece of music. You can RELAX, Your copyright is protected automatically. Just email your work to a friend so you can prove when you created it.

BRANDING ➔ TRADEMARKS

You have created a logo or a brand name for your business and don't want other people copying it. Well, for a fee you can register it as a trademark, which will stop other people from using it. But it is probably wiser to first save your money and register your brand only once your business is showing signs of real success,

THE APPEARANCE OF A PRODUCT ➔ DESIGN PATENT

The appearance of your product is not automatically protected in the United States, so to protect your design, you should register it. You can RELAX a little, because other people won't be able to just copy the look, shape, and feel of your design right away. But remember, you probably have only a year in which to register your design after going public. See uspto.gov for more information from the United States Patent and Trademark Office.

AN INVENTION ➔ PATENTS

You've invented a new product or process? DO NOT RELAX. You should apply for a **patent** *before* telling the world about it. That way, competitors won't be able to copy your invention for 20 years. Edison famously patented the lightbulb although he wasn't the first to invent it. And that patent, along with more than 1,000 others, helped him become one of the richest men in the United States.

IS IT AN ORIGINAL INVENTION?

The trouble with inventions is that it is not always clear whether your idea is a truly new invention. If you think you might have invented something new, what next? Can you get a patent? And how?

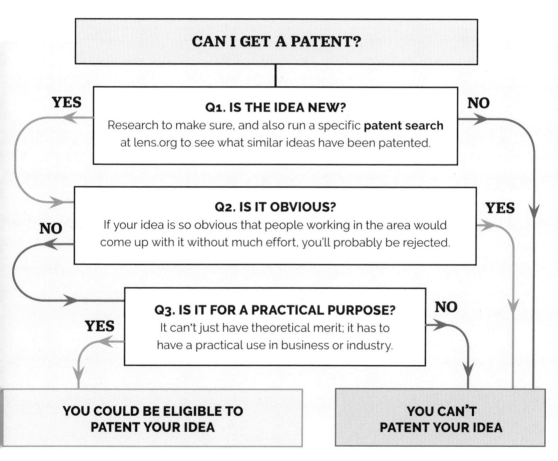

CAN I GET A PATENT?

YES

Q1. IS THE IDEA NEW?
Research to make sure, and also run a specific **patent search** at lens.org to see what similar ideas have been patented.

NO

Q2. IS IT OBVIOUS?
If your idea is so obvious that people working in the area would come up with it without much effort, you'll probably be rejected.

NO

YES

Q3. IS IT FOR A PRACTICAL PURPOSE?
It can't just have theoretical merit; it has to have a practical use in business or industry.

YES

NO

YOU COULD BE ELIGIBLE TO PATENT YOUR IDEA

YOU CAN'T PATENT YOUR IDEA

If you think you might have invented something new, then check the U.S. government's patent website (uspto.gov) for the appropriate information or ask for advice. One recommended way, especially if you're still not completely sure whether your product idea should be patented, is to get an information pack from innovate-design.com and apply online for a free review of your idea.

Use It

Spending Fears

Money is hard to get but easy to use, right? *Wrong.* While having money may open up a world of opportunities, to make the most of those opportunities, you need to know how to use money well.

Most adults learn how to earn money, and there are a lot of books out there on how to grow your wealth. But there's little in the way of guidance when it comes to using money effectively. In fact, many adults end up making mistakes, squandering their wealth, and then become uncertain about money matters.

Some people end up growing so anxious about money that it keeps them up at night. Did you know that according to an international poll carried out by the magazine *Reader's Digest*, money is the number one reason for stress in most countries?

The most common mistake people make is spending money on inessential stuff (which ultimately doesn't lead to happiness) or falling for a scam or buying stuff that encourages human or animal suffering or causes harm to the planet.

It's like you're walking through a minefield!

But, by learning how to avoid the pitfalls and instead creating a smart and mature relationship with money, you can gain the freedom to do what you want and, yes, money can ultimately lead to happiness!

If you are ready to navigate the money minefield, probably the place to start is learning to recognize the difference between **Want** and **Need**.

Want Vs. Need?

Generally speaking, a "need" is something you absolutely cannot live without. A "want," on the other hand, is something you would like to have but could probably live without if push comes to shove.

The more money we have to spend, the easier it is to manage this relationship as we have more left for the things we want once out needs have been met. But if money is tight, or you're still trying to grow your wealth, it is important to think ahead before making a spending decision. Do I really need this (now) or do I just want it?

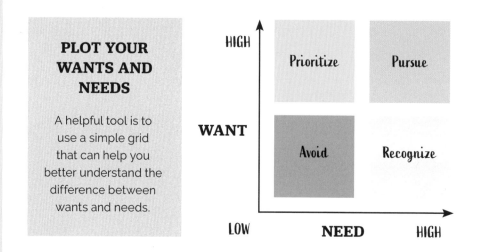

PLOT YOUR WANTS AND NEEDS

A helpful tool is to use a simple grid that can help you better understand the difference between wants and needs.

Some things can be simple. If a laptop is a "High Need" for homework and a "High Want" for watching YouTube videos, then you *PURSUE* it.

You might identify and *AVOID* habitual spending on things you don't need or even want that much, such as an old magazine subscription.

If there's something you want but don't need, it doesn't mean you must do without it. Instead, think about whether it is something you want to *PRIORITIZE*. Ask yourself how you can afford that new phone, for example, and what work you are willing to do to earn the money to be able to buy it.

And there are always things you need but don't really want to spend money on, such as new lights for your bike. *RECOGNIZING* when something is truly needed can be important.

Try plotting the following items on the grid by considering whether they are essential or just nice to have:

- PET POODLE • UNDERPANTS
- SEASON TICKET TO FOOTBALL
- SCHOOLBAG • FERRARI 250 GTO
- LIMITED EDITION SNEAKERS
- DRINKING WATER

Now try something a little harder. Think about the **last three things** you spent money on. Try plotting those items on the grid.

THE DRIVE TO BUY

Did you find the exercise easy or hesitate with some of the items? It is a challenge to be truly honest and put something in the nice-to-have-but-not-essential category when you really want it. However, the desire to have things is often what drives us to work hard in pursuit of them, so it's good to aspire to wanting things you currently don't have but dream of owning. As our circumstances change, so do our needs and desires. Something that seems important to you now, may not feel so in the future.

But once you start looking more closely at the things you buy, you'll quickly find that most of them are things you don't need—they're things you want. And understanding *why* we want them is a major step to achieving financial freedom in the long run.

So, what drives us to spend? **Why do we buy the things we buy?**

Why Do We Buy the Things We Buy?

Why do we buy that vintage sweatshirt that costs double its original price? Or that new car that drops in value as soon as we drive it out of the showroom?

"**D**opamine made me do it" is the short answer. It is the same reason lab rats can spend their lives licking a sugar feed.

DON'T BLAME ME! THE DOPAMINE MADE ME DO IT.

Yeah sure, we can blame the ads, or the vlogger, or the cool kid at school who always has trendier stuff than us. We can even sometimes kid ourselves into believing that we *need* the things we want, but the underlying cause—the chemical messenger that drives most of our spending—is dopamine.

Dopamine is sometimes called the "feel-good hormone" but, in fact, it is only one of many brain chemicals that makes us feel good.

We get a dopamine boost whenever we check our social media or eat our favorite food. And, *critically*, we get a dopamine hit when we **buy stuff**. We even get a dopamine hit watching someone else unboxing stuff (remember Evan the YouTube influencer on page 31—he has made a fortune out of convincing you to buy stuff he likes).

FUN BUT FLEETING

We have evolved to chase the dopamine hit, because it drives the kind of novelty-seeking behavior that helped humans survive and flourish through the ages. Now, in the twenty-first century, it is what propels us to keep checking our phone and spending money on things that aren't essential. It is also what drives us to earn money and be successful. So, dopamine has both a good and bad side, and finding the right balance is key.

The problem with dopamine is that it is a short-term happiness chemical. It's the **"Quick Fix Happy Hormone"** and is designed (evolved) to disappear quickly. No matter what caused that dopamine to increase, be it a new pair of flashy sneakers, a new car, or even a new house, it will always return to that baseline level. And it happens surprisingly quickly.

And so chasing the dopamine rush can never lead to long-term happiness.

HOW LONG DOES THE DOPAMINE HIT LAST?

YOUR FAVORITE FOOD
About 10 minutes

A NEW CAR
A few minutes a day for a month or two

A NEW HOUSE
A few minutes a day for a few months

For 99 percent of purchases, any effect on happiness lasts less than a few hours.

SOCIAL PRESSURES

Sometimes we envy things that others have and think we would be happier if we had those things, too. We also crave the status that stuff brings; we want the attention, we want to feel like a success. Be honest with yourself; what do you crave and why? Does that vintage T-shirt really bring you joy? Or is it mainly the social kudos it brings? And is that old phone really too slow? Or do you mainly want the joy of feeling like a winner with a new phone?

So, how do you stop yourself from giving in to the pressures of society? The first step is to simply notice the dopamine effect and how quickly the joy wears off after you buy something. Step two is to figure out what your spending weaknesses are and whether there are any outside pressures driving these habits.

Money Can Make You Happy

So, dopamine is the short-term happiness chemical in our brain, but are there any long-term happiness chemicals? And what about chemicals that make us unhappy and we need to dodge?

L et's look at an *un*happiness chemical first. **Cortisol** is the stress hormone that is the body's inbuilt alarm system. A little cortisol is useful, because it motivates us to take action. For example, we get a cortisol surge to help us perform when we are about to take a test. But for most people in the twenty-first century, including kids, cortisol is too high for too much of the time, making us chronically stressed.

Your T-shirt is embarrassing

You scored an F in math

Your friends have a Whatsapp group you're not part of

Your MOM started following you on Snapchat

Is that a zit coming up?

HOW MONEY CAN HELP

Stresses generally tend to grow in adulthood as we take on more responsibilities and expose ourselves to the many shocks, crises, and anxieties of life. This is where having enough money can save us from the chronic flood of cortisol. If, for example, a person can afford time off when they are sick or can afford a physio if they are injured or can buy a new phone if theirs gets stolen, they can spare themselves from the worry that any of these situations creates.

But that's only the half of it. Money gives you the freedom to do stuff that *really* makes you happy. And real happiness releases a whole bunch of other brain chemicals that can alter your brain for the better. They are the **long-term happiness hormones.** There are a lot of things you can do to boost these, and some don't cost a penny. Hug your mom (or anybody you are close to) regularly and it will boost oxytocin levels in your brain. Eating a relaxed meal with friends or family will do the same. Time spent outdoors in nature and exercise boost endorphins, serotonin, and endocannabinoids—all feel-good chemicals.

FLOW STATE

But there's one happy brain state that beats all the rest. Psychologists call it FLOW. Flow is a state of peak enjoyment that occurs when you are doing something that is difficult and you are highly skilled at. It's those moments of rapt attention and total immersion in a task. Life is as good as it gets when you are in a flow state.

How do you achieve flow? Different people achieve flow by engaging in different activities. You might achieve it while coding, drawing, or dancing. But there's one way to guarantee you'll achieve it—that is to create something you are passionate about. It could be a business, a piece of art, an ornate flower border, or a graphic novel. The truth is, however, most adults cannot immerse themselves in the act of creating, because they are too busy working to earn money. That's where financial freedom can provide you the freedom to create.

Rising from Financial Ruin

We have heard stories of lottery winners who have ended up broke a few years down the line, squandering their winnings on fancy cars, bad investments, or by employing questionable accountants. But how familiar are you with the tales of some of the brightest and most successful people on the planet who have also lost it all?

The difference between the bankrupt lottery winners and the unfortunate entrepreneurs who lost all their hard-earned riches is that the second lot have often been able to build back their wealth. Here are a few stories of tycoons who have been through that exact journey to rise from financial ruin.

MARTHA STEWART

"Without an open-minded mind, you can never be a great success."

Retail businesswoman Martha Stewart was America's first, self-made female billionaire. However, in 2004, she was sent to prison for insider trading (unfairly making money on the public stock exchange using information that others do not have access to). After serving her time, Stewart returned to lead her company back into big profit within a year.

JAMES ALTUCHER

"Luck is created by the prepared."

In 1996, James Altucher founded a web-design company called Reset Inc. Just two years later he sold it for $10 million. However, thereafter he made some bad investment decisions during the first "tech bubble" and lost all that money. Altucher had to start all over again. He took a job as a hedge-fund manager, worked hard, and also became a popular blogger and podcaster. As of 2021, he is worth $20 million.

YASUMITSU SHIGETA

"The slightest delay in judgment or decision-making will outdate the idea itself right then and there."

Japan's Yasumitsu Shigeta started his cell phone company Hikari Tsushin in 1988, at just 23 years old. By 2000, he was worth $42 billion, with his wealth fluctuating by as much as $5 billion a day due to the seesawing nature of the tech boom. When the Japanese IT bubble burst later that year, Shigeta's company lost almost $41 billion, wiping out his fortune in a matter of weeks. Since that low, Shigeta has worked hard to rebuild his business and, as of 2021, he is estimated to be worth $4.9 billion, making him the ninth richest man in Japan.

Learning how to avoid financial ruin from these people is a good start, but there are other pitfalls when it comes to using money. It is surprisingly easy to spend money on stuff that does harm. Thankfully, you can avoid that, too. Let's take a look.

Spending Ethically

Did that money you spent on sneakers help fund a sweatshop? Does the factory that made your favorite sweatshirt also dump microplastics into the ocean? And what about the moisturizer you use daily—was it tested on animals? If so, maybe it's time to consider where your cash is going before you part with it?

BUT IT'S ONLY LIP BALM.

Tested on a mouse

Plastic ends up in a landfill

Factory workers are paid a paltry wage

Transported from China using diesel

Before you start screaming for forgiveness, remember you don't have to be perfect. Anything you do to improve the ethics of your spending will do some good, plus it can also result in you making sound financial decisions. Think about it. Buying items secondhand or reusing stuff, for example, costs less. Here are a few hints and tips to get you started:

TOP TIPS

1
BUY LESS
Don't fall prey to fast fashion.
Avoid buying new and first try fixing
the old; go to ifixit.com for advice
and guides.

2
BUY SECONDHAND
Go vintage.
Source used items
from such sites as Ebay
and Depop.

3
CUT THE CARBON
Buy food that is grown locally.
Take fewer vacations abroad
but go for longer.
Eat less meat.

4
CHECK THE BRAND
Use an app, such as goodonyou.eco,
to find out how eco-conscious a fashion
label is. Check other brands at
ethicalconsumer.org.

5
RENT IT INSTEAD
Before you buy, check fatllama.com
to see if you can rent it instead
And rent out your own stuff so
other people buy less!

6
REUSE
Drink from a reusable
water bottle.
Search for "zero waste"
alternatives.

7
DON'T TRASH IT!
Sell it on Ebay, give it to
trashnothing.com, or go to
upcyclethat.com to reuse it.

Don't Get Scammed

With most of us shopping online nowadays, we are bombarded with advertisements tempting us to click and buy. Our browsing history helps to drive the algorithms behind what ads we see, so it is no surprise that if we are interested in a particular product, we will see more ads for it than anything else. While shopping online is easy and convenient, it can also be risky.

It pays to be more careful when making an online purchase than if you were buying the same item from a store at the shopping mall. When things go wrong with an online purchase, it can be harder to track down the seller to get the problem fixed. What's more, sometimes online stores are scams with fake email addresses or phone numbers and they exist only to rob you of your money. Here are some pointers on how to protect yourself when you are shopping online.

WAYS TO SHOP SMART ONLINE

1 Only buy from recognized sellers and, where possible, go to the site via a search engine instead of typing the name of the store in your browser bar. The smallest typo could land you on the wrong site and, before you know it, you could be handing your credit card details and personal information into the wrong hands.

2 If sharing any personal information online, including payment details, try to avoid doing so on public Wi-Fi. Shop from home—unless you know how to use a Virtual Private Network (VPN).

4 Watch out for email scams enticing you with incredible offers. Sometimes scammers use the name of someone you know, but the email is sent from a unrecognizable address. And, of course, never open email attachments or clink on links if you don't know the sender or it seems suspicious.

3 Use a credit card instead of a debit card to pay. Credit cards offer better fraud protection, because the credit card company has equal responsibility as the seller for anything you buy. So, in the event you get scammed, or the goods just don't turn up for whatever reason, contact the credit card company and they will help to investigate and usually refund the full amount.

5 Scammers are known to set up fake e-commerce sites. Before making a purchase, read reviews to hear what others say about the seller. In addition, look for a physical location and any customer-service information. It's also a good idea to call the seller to confirm that they are legitimate.

What can you do if you fall prey to a scam? File a complaint on usa.gov/stop-scams-frauds, the government's website for reporting a range of scams and fraud, from fake checks and sweepstakes offers to IRS imposters and disaster scams. It provides links to your local state consumer protection office as well as to the federal government.

How to Manage Your Money

It takes both time and hard work to grow your stash of money so, once you have it, you should do your best to look after it. Money can disappear really quickly if you adopt a carefree attitude. One way to manage your money is to keep a track of how much you have and how you're spending it.

How many times have you thought that you can't live without buying something, or that an item is priced so cheaply that it would be criminal not to buy it? It's easy to make silly spending decisions. Among the best ways to stop spending money frivolously is to formulate a plan that balances the money that is coming in (income) with money that is going out (expenses)—this is known as budgeting.

HOW TO BUDGET

The first step is to write down how much money you have. Then write down how much money you expect to earn or receive each month. Finally, list all the things you must pay for every month (you can do it weekly, if you prefer).

Keep track of how much you spend. By doing so, you will always know exactly how much money you have leftover. Ideally, you want to be earning more than you spend each week/month, so that you can continue growing your wealth. The goal is to try to grow it a little more each month through earning and carefully managing your outgoings. It is also sensible to keep extra cash for emergencies or investment opportunities that might come up.

If you want a little help getting started, why not download a budgeting app? One of the best things you can do for your financial future is to start learning good personal-finance habits, and these apps can help fast track your financial literacy knowledge.

THE PERFECT BUDGET

There is no such thing as the ideal budget. Every person has their own set of wants and needs that will determine how they allocate their funds every week or month. Ultimately, the ideal budget is one you will probably stick to. However, to give yourself a starting point, you could try the 50/30/20 model, where 50 percent of your income goes toward needs, 30 percent toward wants, and the remainder toward savings and debt repayment. See how you get on and make adjustments, if necessary.

Ways to Pay for the Things You Want

When it comes to making payments, knowing what options you have will help you make the most of your money and will also make you feel more in control of your finances. Let's look at some of these payment methods and the pros and cons of each one.

BARTER, THE REALLY OLD-FASHIONED WAY

Bartering is the act of trading one thing for another without using money. The items that are traded are usually worth the same amount of money. Bartering was common practice in prehistoric times, when money did not exist in the wide form it does now. While bartering is rare nowadays, you can still use it to get what you want. If you have something that someone wants and they have something you want, then do a swap. Imagine the money you could be saving.

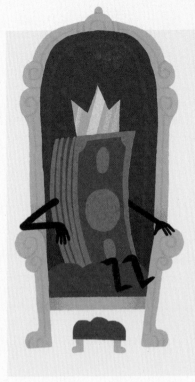

IS CASH KING?

The advantage of cash is that it is money in hand, ready to spend. If, for example, you have invested a lot of your savings in shares or real estate, you'll need to sell these assets to get access to your funds. There's also no danger of spending more than you have with cash. There are of course risks with cash, too. Cash can be stolen or lost and, if this happens, it can be difficult or impossible to recover. While credit cards provide some protection against fraud, once you make a cash payment for an item or service, and if you don't have a written contract or receipt, there's not a lot you can do to get your money back if something goes wrong with the purchase. Cash can also get grubby and germy over time and unpleasant to handle.

PAYING WITH PLASTIC

Cards—whether credit, debit, or prepaid—are easy to carry and you can use them abroad, meaning you don't have to change money into the local currency. Credit cards can offer protection against fraud when you use them to make a purchase. The danger, however, is that the chances are greater that you'll spend more than necessary using a card, because it somehow does not feel like real money. Handing over cash is always harder so, if you're in the habit of overspending, a credit card can spell trouble. Remember, too, that while debit and prepaid cards directly run down the money in the bank account or on the card, credit cards do not. They are a form of "unsecured debt," meaning that there is a risk that you could spend more than you can afford.

THE DANGERS OF USING A CREDIT CARD

1. If you can't pay off the full balance every month, you will have to pay interest on the remaining balance, and the credit card interest charge (known as the Annual Percentage Rate or APR) is expensive, around 25 percent or more. This means you owe even more, making it harder to pay back.

2. If you run into trouble paying off your credit card, it could affect your credit rating. This is how companies score you to decide how much they can lend you the next time you want to borrow money, for example, to buy a car or a house. A bad credit rating makes getting future credit (or borrowing) more expensive or impossible, which could have a lasting impact as you get older.

3. There can be hidden charges on every transaction you make, if you use the card outside of your country. Some credit cards also charge an annual membership fee.

SMART PHONE PAYMENTS

Using your cell phone to pay for things first became popular in poorer countries, such as Kenya and Bangladesh, where secure ATM networks are located only in the cities. This payment method is now available around the world. The only hitch is that you still need a bank account to be able to make smart phone payments. Nevertheless, smart phone payments will probably eventually take over from credit and debit cards altogether, because it is easier and cheaper.

CRYPTOCURRENCY

Cryptocurrency is a type of digital money that lets people make payments directly to each other through an online system. The use of cryptocurrency is still limited, but many experts believe it could become the most accepted form of money in the future. The most well-known cryptocurrency is Bitcoin, which was the first cryptocurrency that came into the digital currency market in 2008.

The reason many people like cryptocurrency is because it isn't controlled by anyone—unlike a fiat currency, which is printed and controlled by a country's central bank. Because cryptocurrrencies don't have a "fixed value" set by law, their worth is decided by what people are willing to pay for them. This makes cryptocurrency a high-risk and volatile asset. Nevertheless, many people actually buy cryptocurrency as a form of investment instead of as a means to buy and sell things. This is commonly known as crypto trading.

TRADING IN BITCOIN

Since it was first introduced to the world more than a decade ago, Bitcoin has had a volatile trading history. In the early days, Bitcoin traded for a fraction of a penny. The price peaked at around $20,000 in 2017, but two years later had plunged to $7,100. By late 2021, Bitcoin had again reached an all-time high of almost $67,000.

I'd Like to Open a Bank Account

So your money jar is overflowing. Now where do you keep your cash? The obvious answer is to take it to a bank. A person who has money deposited in a bank is said to have a bank account.

WHY USE A BANK ACCOUNT?

Your money is safe once you move it to a bank—banks keep their money in secure vaults and use sophisticated computer systems that ensure hackers can't break in and commit robbery electronically. Once you open a bank account, the bank keeps a track of your spending and saving and records this in a bank statement.

If you open a **bank account** (see page 108), you'll receive a debit card giving you access to your money; you can pay for things using the card or use it to withdraw cash from the bank's ATM. You can also pay for things with your phone by uploading an electronic version of your debit card onto it.

If you put your money into a **savings account** (see page 108), your money can earn you interest. This is an additional amount—calculated as a percentage—that the bank pays you for saving with them. Remember, banks are businesses, too, and they invest your money to make money themselves, so it's only fair that they pay you for letting them use your money.

BANK CHARGES

If you spend more money than you have, you will be "overdrawn" and may have to pay interest and charges. There are charges for other services, too, for example, if you want to withdraw money from another bank's cash machines or if you want to send or receive money from abroad. When opening an account, it is sensible to ask the bank what you might get charged for to avoid any unpleasant surprises.

WAYS TO AVOID CHARGES

1. Know your balance. Check your account often to keep track of your money, and to avoid it dropping below the minimum deposit needed to avoid fees.
2. Use online or mobile banking to check your account easily.
3. Make sure you know when money is coming in and going out of your account, for example, your regular payments each month.
4. If you're experiencing financial difficulties, speak to the bank—it may be able to help.

TYPES OF BANK ACCOUNTS

Checking accounts give you ready access to your money so that you can manage your spending with ease. Consider one that can be assessed online for ease of banking. Some offer an annual percentage yield (APY) if you leave a large enough deposit in the account.

Savings accounts are intended for money that you can leave in for a period of time. Many people use them to keep emergency funds or to grow money to buy something expensive. The interest rate may be low but they usually offer a better APY than a checking account.

Certificate of Deposits (CDs) generally offer a higher rate of interest than a regular savings account. These accounts are used to hold and grow money over a longer period. If you have a sum of money that you don't need anytime soon, leave it in your CD account to earn interest securely.

HOW TO CALCULATE BANK INTEREST

Bank of Maxx is offering 1.5 percent interest per year on their savings accounts, and 3 percent per year on their deposit accounts. If you deposit $1,000 in the savings account and $1,000 in the deposit account, how much interest would you earn if you kept your money in the bank for one complete year?

SAVINGS ACCOUNT

$1,000
x 0.015
= $15

C ACCOUNT

$1,000
x 0.03
=$30

WHAT IS THE FOREIGN EXCHANGE RATE?

Ellie is an entrepreneur who starts selling her products to Hong Kong and receives payment in Hong Kong dollars. On arrival to her U.S. bank account, the money needs to be converted into U.S. dollars. Because she is planning to do a lot of business with other countries, it makes sense for her to have a multicurrency bank account so she can decide when to change the foreign currency into U.S. dollars. Exchange rates are important to understand, because they never stay the same. The value of currencies—relative to one another—changes all the time. Ideally, Ellie would want to swap her Hong Kong dollars for U.S. dollars when the value of the Hong Kong dollar is high, so she gets more U.S. dollars per Hong Kong dollar.

	WE BUY AT	WE SELL AT
USD	5.56	5.64
EUR	3.01	3.45
JPY	5.67	9.02
GBP	7.23	5.67

UNDERSTANDING EXCHANGE RATES

Bank of Maxx is offering the following exchange rates for 1 U.S. dollar:

	June	July
Australian dollar	1.3259	1.3487
Canadian dollar	1.2035	1.2769
Chinese yuan	6.0421	6.1829
Czech koruna	22.4176	22.7526
Danish krone	6.6061	6.7405

To calculate how many of each currency you would receive for one U.S. dollar, just multiply your one dollar by the number shown against each currency. For example, you would get 1.3259 Australian dollars for each U.S. dollar you exchange in June.

How many Chinese yuan could you expect to receive for 100 U.S. dollars? And would you be better exchanging U.S. dollars for Danish krone in June or July?

Fake Cash

Ever since money came into use in the ancient world, criminals have tried, sometimes successfully, to copy money illegally. The practice is known as counterfeiting, and its effect on the economy can be disastrous, because it reduces the value of real currency. Paper money is the most popular product counterfeited. Over the years, government currency printers have devised more sophisticated ways to make it difficult for a forger to produce fake cash.

KNOW YOUR CASH IS REAL

All bank notes will carry a serial number, which is the easiest way for banks to determine whether a note is real. To do this, they have sophisticated tools such as currency verification and processing machines (CVPS) to check the numerical accuracy and genuineness of a banknote. However, for us, here are a few tips on how to check whether your banknote is real or fake:

WATERMARKS
Many banknotes will feature a watermark that is visible from either side of the banknote when held up to the light.

COLOR-SHIFTING INK
Look for ink that changes color when the banknote is tilted slightly. On the $100 U.S. note, there is an inkwell design that changes from copper to green.

SECURITY THREADS
Many banknotes have a clear thread that is embedded vertically into the paper. The thread is inscribed with the denomination of the note and is visible only when held to the light. It also glows when a UV light is shone upon it.

3-D SECURITY RIBBON
Some banknotes have a ribbon woven into the paper. When you tilt the note back and forth, some images move side to side. Then, if you tilt the banknote side to side, they move up and down.

With all the technology that goes into making banknotes, have you ever wondered whether it costs more than $1 to make the $1 note?

MASTER FAKER

In 2008, Canadian Frank Bourassa spent $300,000 on materials and made $250 million in fake $20 U.S. dollar bills. He was caught in 2012, but incredibly spent just six weeks in prison despite his counterfeit organization being the biggest ever to be run by one man.

The Beauty of Giving

People give to charity for all types of reasons. For some, it is customary; for others, it is a religious duty. There are also those who give to a specific charity because of a life experience. Maybe they were living on the streets at one time so now want to help the homeless or experienced an illness and now support a charity that is researching into potential treatments.

Did you know that people who donate to charity or do charitable acts generally become happier the more they give? They tend to live longer, too. Maybe Bill Gates and Warren Buffet—two of the world's richest men—knew that when they decided to give away their fortunes (see page 118).

Still not convinced? You might be interested to learn that a brain scan experiment conducted on volunteers in Japan revealed that the pleasure and reward centers of their brains lit up more on giving their money away when compared to receiving it.

GET INVOLVED IN GIVING

Why not see for yourself if you can experience the happiness that comes from giving to others? But how do you decide which cause to give to? The first step is about identifying the reason for giving that feels important to you.

CHOOSE A CAUSE THAT IS . . .

...CLOSEST TO YOUR HEART

Find a cause that feels personal to you. Maybe a grandparent is being helped by a senior citizen charity or maybe you feel strongly about the planet or wildlife or education in the developing world. Write down three causes you might be interested in.

...TRYING TO TACKLE A BIG ISSUE

Target a big problem by supporting a cause that could potentially help millions. For example, malaria kills a child every 30 seconds globally. So, supporting the Against Malaria Foundation could have a huge impact.

...GUARANTEED TO HAVE AN IMPACT

Your donation will have an immediate impact if you choose a cause where headway is already being made. For example, the simple technology already exists to help millions around the world who don't have proper access to clean water. Clean water charities can easily provide faucets and toilets with the money they receive.

...LESS WELL-KNOWN

Charities for children and animals already attract billions of donations. Maybe your money could go to a less popular cause that really needs it. Little-known charities have to work much harder to raise money, so any donation you make will probably be used as effectively as possible.

Effective Giving

Did you know there is a difference between how well charities use the donations they receive? According to the altruism organization givingwhatwecan.org, some charities are tens, hundreds, or even a thousand times more effective than others. So, as well as choosing a cause you believe in, it's important to see which charity will make the most difference with your donation.

L et's say you wanted to donate $100 to help improve school attendance of poor children in developing countries. One charity chooses to use the money to pay for scholarships while the other intends to fund a deworming program, which involves giving medicine to children to rid them of parasitic worms.

So, which initiative would result in children statistically spending additional years in school?

PAY FOR A SCHOLARSHIP	**Vs**	**DEWORMING TREATMENT**

Statistics reveal that providing $100 for merit scholarships results in about **70 days** of school attendance.

A $100 donation to the SCI Foundation for school-based deworming treatments translates into about **20 years** of extra school attendance for children, because it reduces absence through sickness.

Moreover, the deworming program reduces child deaths, improves health over a lifetime, and increases lifetime earnings by more than $1,000!

CHOOSE WISELY

So, you've decided which cause you want to help. Now, make a short list of three different charities that support the cause. Look at their websites to see how they help. Look up their "impact report" online. The report will set out exactly what they achieve with the money they receive. If you're still in doubt, check: givingwhatwecan.org, givewell.org, and founderspledge.com. These sites do the work for you and sum up how effective the charities are with an **Impact Score**.

If you gave $8.50 a month for a year to three different charities helping some of the world's poorest people, what statistical impact would each make on the recipient's lifespan?

NEW INCENTIVES	**AGAINST MALARIA FOUNDATION**	**HELEN KELLER INTERNATIONAL**
Funds vaccination programs in Nigeria.	Provides insecticidal nets to regions with the highest cases of the disease.	Works to prevent blindness and fight malnutrition globally.

$100 gets two families vaccinated against childhood diseases. **1.5 extra years of life!**	$100 gets 20 mosquito nets delivered. **1 extra year of life!**	$100 gets vitamin A supplements delivered. **2 extra years of life!**

DO YOUR RESEARCH

It is tempting to give to the charities that claim to have the lowest overheads—the money that they spend on staff and collecting donations. But research shows that these charities often have the lowest impact. You're better off looking at what the charity achieves with its money. The best charities collect evidence of what they achieve, so look for the evidence.

Max Your Giving

So, you've done your research and chosen the charity that will use your donation most effectively. But did you know there are also ways to take your giving to the next level?

Remember that $100 given to the SCI Foundation for treating parasitic worms? It led to 20 years more education, because vulnerable kids could now attend school. Well, what if you could turn that into 80 years more schooling?

GIVE $100

= 20 YEARS OF SCHOOLING

Treating parasitic worms in sub-Saharan Africa is one of the most cost-effective ways of improving people's lives. In addition to saving lives, improving health, and increasing wealth, the $100 donation brings about 20 years of extra education.

DOUBLE IT TO $200 = 40 YEARS OF SCHOOLING

You could double your money with matching funds. Some companies and foundations agree to match the amount you donate. Booker T. Washington had a millionaire friend who funded projects to help black Americans that had partial matching funds.

INCREASING IT TO $400 = 80 YEARS OF SCHOOLING

How about getting help from a parent or other adult? Ask an adult if his or her employer has an employee matching gift incentive. By getting that adult to make a $100 donation on your behalf, it will be matched by his or her company. And you can do even better—tell the adult what you're doing and why. Ask him or her to increase it with a $100 gift of his or her own and suddenly you're up to $400!

BOOMERANG GIVING

What if you could get your donation back and then give it to someone else? Well you can. It's called Microfinancing. Platforms such as **lendwithcare.org** allow for you to *invest* in people and businesses in developing countries. It turns giving into investing and many see the benefit in promoting self-sufficiency and independence. They see loans creating sustainable businesses that will have an impact long after the loan is paid back. Here's how it works:

ANGELITA FROM THE PHILIPPINES

Needs: $4,000 to fund her farm vehicle business.

The business: She buys old, broken farm vehicles and fixes them up to sell on to local farmers. She employs her two sons and four other local mechanics.

Why she needs the money: The business is new and growing. She needs capital to scale up and buy more broken vehicles to fix up.

The impact: Employing more mechanics, reusing more broken vehicles destined for the scrap pile, and increasing the productivity of local farmers.

The Big Givers

The practice of giving away your money is known as philanthropy and, when done well, it can be extremely impactful. Here are some of the world's most famous humanitarians, past and present, who have donated vast sums of their wealth.

BILL GATES AND WARREN BUFFET

To date, the founder of Microsoft, Bill Gates, has donated around $36 billion. As Microsoft began to take off, Gates set up his own foundation to find ways to improve the lives of the impoverished. Over the years, he has also worked with other influential leaders, but most often the equally successful Warren Buffet—the founder of the investment company Berkshire Hathaway—to create a superpower foundation. Interestingly, Buffet had always maintained that he would not give away any of his wealth but had a change of heart in 2006, when he pledged more than $30 billion to Gates's foundation. Together, they also created the Giving Pledge, which now has more than 70 wealthy individuals and families committed to giving away their fortune to help others.

MARK ZUCKERBERG

In 2015, Facebook founder Mark Zuckerberg, together with his wife Priscilla Chan, created the Chan Zuckerberg Initiative, which is funded by 99 percent of their combined wealth from their shares in Facebook. CZI's main focus is funding work in science and education, as well as promoting housing affordability, criminal justice reform, and immigration reform. In 2016, they launched the Chan Zuckerberg Science program, with a $3 billion investment over the next 10 years. Their aim is to help cure, manage, or prevent all disease by the year 2100. More recently, CZI has invested money into trying to understand coronavirus, following the global pandemic in 2020.

JAMSETJI TATA

Jamsetji Tata (1839–1904) was an Indian pioneer industrialist who founded the Tata Group. He is widely viewed as the "Father of Indian Industry," having made such an impact during his life, specifically in the field of iron and steel production. Tata was the biggest giver in the world, not only in the last century but also this century, in relative terms. His donations have been valued in modern-day terms as a whopping $102 billion—more than that of Gates and Buffet combined. His principle was to give away two-thirds of everything he owned to companies or charities that were engaged in doing good, be it education or healthcare, with his first donation made in 1892.

The 7 Secrets to Max Your Money

There is a lot in this book, but hopefully you now know how to **earn** more, **grow** your money, and **use it** in a way that will give you financial freedom and make you happier. We reckon the information can be summed up into seven **key guiding principles** that are guaranteed to boost your wealth, health, and happiness. If you ever need a reminder, here they are.

7 SECRETS TO MAX YOUR MONEY

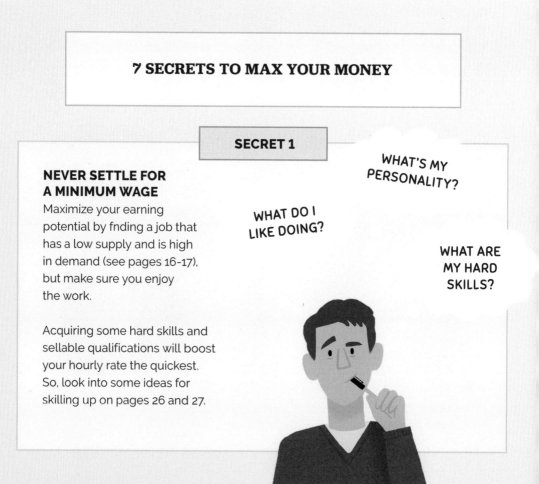

SECRET 1

NEVER SETTLE FOR A MINIMUM WAGE

Maximize your earning potential by fnding a job that has a low supply and is high in demand (see pages 16-17), but make sure you enjoy the work.

Acquiring some hard skills and sellable qualifications will boost your hourly rate the quickest. So, look into some ideas for skilling up on pages 26 and 27.

WHAT'S MY PERSONALITY?

WHAT DO I LIKE DOING?

WHAT ARE MY HARD SKILLS?

SECRET 2

TODAY THE NYSE
ROSE 2 POINTS.

CHOOSE THE RIGHT JOB

Match your career to your personality (see pages 22-23). Do not be the creative soul who becomes trapped in the body of an accountant. Remember, most adults get it wrong; they end up in jobs and careers that fail to inspire them.

Taking the time to find out what you really want to do can save you years of misery. The effort won't be easy; it means doing personality tests and volunteering to shadow people while they go about their jobs. Whatever you're thinking of training for, first get as much work experience through an internship as you can. And if you do think you've made a mistake, don't get stuck. Work out what will bring you job satisfaction and change your career path.

SECRET 3

FUTURE-PROOF YOURSELF

The job market will change as artificial intelligence and automation take over, making many traditional jobs redundant. The secret to future-proofing yourself is to focus on careers that have a creative aspect to them. Here are some pointers on how to develop your creative muscle.

Be creative If you have a good idea, try to realize it. You might have invented a billion-dollar product or it might be a flop. It doesn't matter. The point is you actioned your idea. And the more you practice that, the more you'll succeed in a fast-changing future.

Be resilient Next time you have a setback, focus on the positives. Try not to walk away, but tell people how you feel and ask for help. Then try again.

Stay playful Remain curious and unafraid when it comes to exploring new things. Whatever change is on the horizon, embrace it head on.

SECRET 4

GROW YOUR MONEY

Make your money work for you—aim to earn as much from your assets as you do from your work. Read the **Grow It** section for the best ways to make your money do some of the heavy lifting. No matter how little money you have, there are always ways to grow it!

SECRET 5

SPEND YOUR MONEY WISELY

The majority of the things you buy, be it a new car or high-fashion outfit, won't make you feel happy for long. The buzz will go after a short while (see page 90).

The key is to become a responsible spender. And if you still *really* want to buy something, the question is not whether you can afford it but how you might be able to afford it. Once you start thinking in this way, two things happen.

First, you begin balancing the money that goes "out" with the money that comes "in" and are prepared to do a little extra work to pay for the extra spending.

Secondly, as a result, some of the magic about buying wears off. People generally crave things that are **out of reach**—so once you know you can get whatever we want (if we work for it), we stop craving things so much.

SECRET 6

SEEK FINANCIAL FREEDOM

We know the dopamine buzz from buying a new iPhone wears off in a few days. But money can protect you from financial stress and avoiding *that* type of stress can have a huge impact on your happiness.

Most important, having money can give you **FREEDOM**! Freedom to avoid horrible bosses and miserable jobs. Freedom from worrying about footing the cost if the furnace breaks down. Freedom to do the things that *really* make you happy: building and creating. Whatever you're inspired to create, having money will free up your time to pursue your passions.

SECRET 7

DEVELOP A CHARITABLE SPIRIT

Acts of charity make people happier, more confident, and even increase their lifespan!

Find a cause that you feel passionate about, research the most effective charities, and maximize your donation (see pages 112-117). And if you can't bear to give money away, lend it to someone in need of capital for their business using a microfinancing platform (see page 117). When you get involved in giving to charity, you'll realize it's one of the best things you've ever done.

Glossary

APR
Annual percentage rate is the cost of the interest rate (see Interest Rate) a person will pay on whatever they are borrowing, for the full year. Interest rates are often shown at their monthly cost.

ASSETS
Something that can be swapped for cash. This might be physical items, such as houses or cars or shares (see Shares) in a company.

BARTER
The act of swapping things without using money; for example, a friend gives you his or her Pokemon cards in exchange for your signed Harry Potter book.

BOOM AND BUST
When an economy of a country is doing well, then moves into a bad spell.

CAPITAL GAINS
The money made after the sale of an asset. For example, if you buy a car for $200 and sell it for $250, your capital gain is $50.

COUNTERPARTY
The person who you enter into a contract or financial transaction with. For example, if you sell your bike to your friend Bobby, then Bobby is the counterparty.

CREDIT CARD
A payment card that lets the cardholder make purchases using borrowed money from the card issuer, normally a bank. You must, however, repay the money used on the card or be charged interest (see Interest).

CRYPTOCURRENCY
A currency (see below) that uses digital files as a form of money. Unlike other currencies, cryptocurrency is not controlled by a government or any single individual.

CURRENCY
Something people use to exchange for goods and services—in short, money. Money can only be created by governments, unless it is a cryptocurrency (see Cryptocurrency) or is fake.

DEBIT CARD
Similar to a credit card (see Credit Card) except that the moment a person buys something with their debit card the money comes straight out of their bank account.

DEBT
A sum of money that is owed to someone by someone else.

DIVIDENDS
When you own shares (see Shares) in a company that makes a profit, it may give

some of the profit to its shareholders. These are known as dividends.

DOT-COM

A company that operates mainly online, through a website. Dot-com refers to the ".com" on a website name.

GEARING

The amount a person borrows compared to how much money they have. Gearing is risky but, when used carefully, it can help you to increase your profits.

HOUSING LADDER

By buying their first house, a person is said to have got onto the housing ladder. When they sell and then buy a more expensive house, they are climbing the housing ladder.

INSURANCE POLICY

An agreement by which a person pays a company and the company promises to pay out money if the person experiences financial loss as a result of unpredictable events, such as accidents and illnesses. The more the policy helps to cover the replacement cost, the more the policy costs.

INTEREST

This is the return a person is paid by a bank to deposit their money in an account. It can also be the price one pays to borrow money. (See APR).

IRA

An individual retirement account allows a person to save for retirement through a financial institution. The contributions can sometimes be deducted on a tax return, and the interest earned might be tax-deferrable until retirement, when the person may be paying a lower tax rate, and therefore save some money.

LIABILITIES

When a person or company owes something—usually money. Examples include loans and mortgages.

LIQUID/ILLIQUID

A person who is "liquid" has a lot of readily available cash. A person who is "illiquid" has their money tied up in assets, such as a house or art collection (see Assets), that are not easily or quickly sellable.

MICROFINANCE

A type of banking service, especially in the form of microloans, provided to impoverished people and groups in poor and developing regions, who struggle to access normal banking services.

MINIMUM WAGE

Decided by governments, the lowest amount an employer can pay an employee. In the United States, the federal minimum wage is $7.50 per hour, but $4.25 per hour for the first 90 consecutive calendar days for employees under 20 years old. State minimum wages may differ.

REAL ESTATE

Property consisting of building and land. Those who invest in real estate buy houses, buildings, or land.

RENTING

The act of paying someone for the use of their asset (see Asset), normally a house, car, or equipment. Renting allows for a person to use something for a period of time without having to buy it.

SECURED DEBT

When a person borrows money from a bank, the bank needs to be sure that the borrower can repay the sum. To "secure" the debt, the borrower "pledges" an asset (see Asset), which the bank can sell in the event the borrower cannot repay the loan.

SHARES

When a company is owned by several people, they are said to have "shares" in the company. These people are known as shareholders. The price to buy a share in a company is the share price, which moves up and down, depending on how well the company is doing and its stocks are trading.

STOCK EXCHANGE

A system for buying and selling shares (see Shares) in companies. An investor cannot physically go to a stock market to buy shares, so they need someone who works at the stock market (a broker) to buy the shares on their behalf.

TAX

The money people have to pay their government, depending on the money they earn or the assets (see Assets) they own. Taxation is the biggest source of income for governments.

TRADING

The buying and selling of goods and services, from selling underpants at the local store to complex financial products for an investment bank.

VIRTUAL PRIVATE NETWORK (VPN)

A private connection that is used to access a network on the Internet, allowing private data to be sent safely.

VOLATILITY

When something can change quickly and without warning, normally for the worse. This is often used in reference to stock markets (see Stock Markets) or share prices (see Shares).

WEAR AND TEAR

Damage that naturally occurs as a result of usage or age. If a person rents a house or car, there is an accepted level of damage that they would not be expected to fix. What constitutes "wear and tear" should be agreed before an asset is rented.

Index